"As we enter a new century, professional marketers face a new era of communications challenges. Tactics are the same, but the techniques have changed dramatically. *Getting Attention* deserves to get the attention of any marketer who wants to succeed under the new conditions. The numerous case studies presented are relevant to today's technological evolution and bring the potential of these new techniques to life."

—**Stephen Straight,** Chairman 1999–2000, Business Marketing Association

"*Getting Attention* is one of the few books about public relations that displays an accurate, realistic understanding of how reporters think, work, and respond. Communications professionals who read this book will be more effective in getting their message across—and they'll also be more direct and honest in providing reporters with the information the press needs."

—**James Fallows,** author of *Breaking News,* and national correspondent for *The Atlantic Monthly, and columnist for Industry Standard*

"This book contains practical, applicable, and insightful tools to accelerate one's effectiveness in marketing a business and getting attention. It is a great reality check for what you are doing, and what can actually generate significant results. The savings in time and resources will be considerable."

—**Doug Roseborough,** Vice President, Marketing, SmartAge.com

"First down-to-earth how-to primer on how the public relations pro can successfully adapt her/his PR skills to cyberspace. Susan Kohl, APR, has done a great job with *Getting Attention* in creating a 'quick read' that can help any of us navigate the universe too often filled with jargon and geek-speak."

—**Sam Waltz**, APR, CEO & Board Chairman, Public Relations Society of America (PRSA), and President, Sam Waltz & Associates Business & Communications Counsel, Wilmington, Delaware

GETTING ATTENTION

LEADING-EDGE LESSONS FOR PUBLICITY AND MARKETING

GETTING ATTENTION: LEADING-EDGE LESSONS FOR PUBLICITY AND MARKETING

Susan Y. Kohl, APR

Boston Oxford Auckland Johannesburg Melbourne New Delhi

R A member of the Reed Elsevier group

Butterworth–Heinemann supports the efforts of American
Forests and the Global ReLeaf program in its campaign for
the betterment of trees, forests, and our environment.

ISBN 0-7506-7259-5

The publisher offers special discounts on bulk orders of this book.
For information, please contact:
Manager of Special Sales
Butterworth–Heinemann
225 Wildwood Avenue
Woburn, MA 01801–2041
Tel: 781-904-2500
Fax: 781-904-2620
For information on all Butterworth–Heinemann publications available,
contact our World Wide Web home page at: http://www.bh.com

10 9 8 7 6 5 4 3 2 1

Printed in the United States of America

TABLE OF CONTENTS

ACKNOWLEDGMENTS

Irving Berlin once wrote "The toughest thing about success...is that you have to keep on being a success." I would like to thank the following people for their continued support and personal investments in my success:

To my partner and husband, Doug, for all the things you do for me each and every day, including entertaining our three boys during the writing of this book.

To Frank, Sam, and Max, my greatest achievements, for being such good kids.

To Bill and Rosemary Cloughley, my parents and role models, for always being ready to lend a helping hand.

To Bob and Gwen Tucker, for more than a decade of great friendship.

To Phil Sutherland, Rita Lombard, Scott B. Rousseau, Karen Speerstra, Tina Adoniou, Brian Nelson, Gavor Powers, and Ross R. Olney—for their help and guidance on this project.

To all my family and friends for their love and support.

I thank you all.

FOREWORD

For those of you who don't know me, I have been a correspondent, producer, and anchor with CNN for 15 years at this writing. I met the author in my role as correspondent for The CNN Computer Connection—a television pioneer in the new field of computer technology and Internet reporting. Susan Kohl was the manager of public relations for Metricom, and I was hot on the trail of her company's flagship product, Ricochet—a wireless Internet service conceived in Silicon Valley. In 1997 the prospect of logging onto the Web from the comfort of a San Francisco trolley or Bay ferry seemed like a great story to me. It was a breakthrough I wanted to report to CNN's viewers.

How I learned of Ricochet is interesting: no press packet was delivered in the mail, and no wire service story was released. The tip came by e-mail from an account executive at Metricom's public relations agency. The message grabbed my interest, even though I didn't know the person sending it. I remember the agency woman being helpful and professional and her e-mail conversational, quick, and easy to digest. Best of all, she promised me a great picture story. After several e-mail exchanges, I began to sense that I could trust her to get me the story she promised. So I flew to San Francisco, met Susan and her boss, and produced a piece that got a fair amount of airtime on CNN, which greatly pleased the publicity-conscious folks at Metricom. This was a case of making effective use of the Internet to market a product story to a newsperson. A simple well-written e-mail grew into an "online relationship."

I studied public relations and advertising in college. Advertising seemed an especially exciting excursion through the intricacies of the cognitive human mind. As a student, I was considered promising enough to attract a job offer from the public relations and advertising department of a top Canadian corporation. There was just one problem—similar to many people of my idealistic generation, I was uneasy about the ethics of public relations and advertising. From the ivory tower perspective of academia, these two professions walked the fine gray line between truth and falsehood, often landing in the latter. Psychology—the thing I found so appealing—seemed abused. A noble science transforming consumers into dumb laboratory rats, to be taught to buy what they otherwise wouldn't and believe what they would otherwise distrust. My classmates and I were taught to be contemptuous of the people who practiced these dark arts.

So I turned the job down and became a journalist. A journalist? Frankly, today I often call journalism far more into question than I did (and do) publicity and advertising. Some journalists also tempt gravity in high-wire walks between truth and fiction. Many have hit the ground with bruised professional reputations or damaged careers. Sometimes the mistakes seem so common and serious that critics perceive them as the norm. NBC and even CNN have suffered from accusations of chasing a hot story at the expense of the public's trust, as have several online newspapers.

Trust and relationships are sacred commodities in any profession, but in the anonymity of the Internet, they become vital and increasingly difficult to maintain. To a publicist, the Web offers speed and immediacy in getting a story out. Just as competitive journalists are tempted to skip their homework and run a story, publicists also have to resist the urge to spam. With no stamps to lick, no paper to print, and no mail to send out, that next piece of free publicity could be just a "click" away. I know because I've been spammed a lot. My revenge? The "DELETE" key, and remembering who spammed me. But Susan Kohl and her agency showed how to do e-mail publicity right. They had a good story, pitched it to a reporter who'd be interested, and provided a personal touch that builds trust.

Technology and the Internet are changing so much of what we do today that at times it's unsettling. But one thing that shouldn't change is how you conduct yourself with journalists and media outlets. In the flurry of fast-paced newsrooms and online newspapers, good reporters need to depend on their sources and their senses more than ever. If their senses tell them they can trust you, then you as a publicist have a size-twelve foot in the door and a willing ear for your story. If their senses tell them otherwise, then it's best to look down at your keyboard and remind yourself just how close the "DELETE" key is.

Brian J. Nelson

CNN anchor and president of Nelson Communications, Inc.

INTRODUCTION

As a marketing and public relations practitioner living in San Jose, California, otherwise known as Silicon Valley, it didn't take me long to realize how fleeting new trends and technologies could be. Overnight one could experience the birth of a technology that promised to be the "next great thing." A few short months later, it would be pronounced dead by media and marketing gurus alike. This new environment of hot and cold technologies, tools, and techniques was a far cry from where I had begun my marketing and public relations career. And it was one that took some time to understand.

Beginning in 1988, I spent almost a decade in a much different high-tech world—NASA's space program. It was a world in which the technology was exciting yet stagnant. As a television and radio journalist, I had participated in more than 50 space shuttle launches since the "return to flight" after the Challenger explosion. Many of the tools and technology had been borrowed from the Apollo days and were simply modified. Surprises were rare, and the only really new technology tended to be associated with the shuttle experiments and space exploration missions. Up until late 1999, space shuttle technology had remained basically the same since its beginnings in 1981.

When I arrived in Silicon Valley in 1996, I felt like I did after watching the first shuttle flight after Challenger. The Internet had been on the scene for a quarter of a century, in one form or another, yet it was just now ready to explode. "Java" and "telephony" were big buzz words in the high-tech world, and Intel had just announced the MMX processor, which was amazing. MMX would incorporate a video accelerator into a chip—a piece of silicon with additional electronic circuitry embedded into it—and promised to expand the possibilities of computing.

It was clear to me that not only would technology change our daily lives, but it would also play a key role in the way we promoted everything, including technology itself. No longer would it be effective to send out a direct mail piece via the United States Postal Service or distribute a press release through the wire services. Technology was changing marketing and public relations practices, and those who did not acknowledge and respond to the changes would be left behind. It was not the world of the space shuttle with its dependable countdown clock and routine launches.

The technology that you will read about in this book, for the most part, is neither expensive nor terribly complex. After being a part of and actually living this high-tech revolution on a daily basis, I have chosen to talk about technologies and marketing and publicity practices that won't be fleeting. Today, these tools and technologies will give you a competitive edge. Tomorrow, they will be commonplace.

I've written this book to help people who may not consider themselves technically savvy or who may be fearful of jumping on board the technology bandwagon. It's written so that the tools and technologies should not be intimidating. This book is practical for people like my sons' swim teacher who is marketing her swimming school on the Web. It's for people like my fellow authors who want to use technology to become self-publicists. It's for public relations practitioners and professional marketers outside of high-tech who want to learn more about the resources available to them. It's for anyone who has a need to communicate and influence the general public—and to get attention.

As you read this book, you will gain some knowledge of the computing industry and learn about the evolution of the Internet and the World Wide Web. You'll find out how to be effective in your publicity and marketing efforts without having the benefit of a large budget or a staff of well-trained professionals. You'll learn some tricks of the trade for breaking through the information overload problem experienced by customers, partners, employees, and the news media.

It's my hope that after reading this book, you'll have more confidence in the choices you make and the activities you pursue for your company, your organization, or yourself. I wish you the utmost success in your endeavors.

THE TWENTIETH CENTURY—THE ADVENTURE BEGINS

The twentieth century. If someone were to ask me what words or phrases I thought best described the twentieth century, I would have to say "an incredible technological adventure." I would focus on technology because it alone has most significantly changed my personal and professional lives. Technology has also changed the world around me, from the way I communicate to the way I'm communicated to.

In the history of the world, we acknowledge that the twentieth century was a relatively short period, yet it encompassed 100 years that produced powerful new technologies, products, and services that enhance our lives today. The twentieth century began with the first-ever radio message sent across the Atlantic Ocean in 1901 and ended with more than 77 million Americans using the Internet. Radio, television, cellular phones, fax machines, pagers, computers, answering machines, VCRs, compact discs, microwave ovens, digital cameras, and electronic mail are all things we take for granted today as we go through our daily lives. Who would have thought that my five-year-old twins would not only know about the Internet but also want to use it regularly?

The speed at which people accepted technology was also amazing. It took radio 30 years to reach 50 million people. It took 10 years for 45 million people to own a personal computer in the United States, but it took less than seven years for 100 million people worldwide to discover and start using the World Wide Web. In 1998 approximately 20 million websites had been created; yet by 1999, search engines were reaching only about 16% of the publicly accessible Web.

There was an incredible amount of information, and all of it was available if you had the right tools. All forms of information—voice, text, and images—were being translated into digital bits. Not only was it being transmitted, but it could also easily be accessed electronically from anywhere, including your home, the workplace, or even from a portable computer. People could now shop, sell goods and services, or conduct transactions, such as banking or trading stocks, online. They could research and book travel through their computers. And they could instantly communicate with friends and strangers from all over the world.

With the phenomenally explosive use of the computer and the Internet, consumers everywhere were becoming increasingly more powerful. Their behavior could and did dictate the success of high-tech–related advertising vehicles such as banner ads, e-mail, and website traffic. With a simple click of a mouse, they either remained on a site or left in search of another one that captivated their attention and gave them a compelling reason to stay. I routinely use the

Internet to do various things, including shopping, and have become critical of commercial sites that are either difficult to navigate or that do not offer me simplicity in the purchase process. I get frustrated with companies that still do not have online catalogs or ordering capability.

MARKETING TOOLS

While the functions of marketing—product development, research, advertising, public relations, and special events—remain somewhat traditional, the methods keep changing. Until the 1970s, almost all marketing was done through traditional vehicles such as the U.S. Postal Service, special events, radio, and television. When companies such as Apple Computer, Radio Shack, and Commodore began a new era by introducing mass-market computers in 1977, things changed. Consumers were warming up to the idea of owning personal computers. In 1984, when the 3.5-inch computer diskette debuted and became industry standard, marketers began to recognize a new vehicle for communicating information to the general public. Massive duplication of computer diskettes, a transportable device on which computer data are stored, and later CD-ROM (Compact Disk, Read-Only Memory) gave them a vehicle for communicating large amounts of information in a relatively inexpensive way. E-mail, the Internet, and the World Wide Web changed the marketing function even more.

Sending marketing collateral and product advertising through the mail has always been an effective way to communicate. It continues to be commonplace for companies to have an artist, graphic designer, or desktop publisher create a dynamic marketing piece, buy a mailing list from a company that specializes in marketing lists, have a fulfillment house lick the stamps, and send the mailing through the U.S. Postal Service. By industry standards, if two percent of a mailing list responded to your call to action, then you had a successful direct marketing campaign. Later, telemarketers would join the activity and pursue sales leads that did not respond immediately to direct mail.

Diskettes and CD-ROM

When diskettes and CD-ROM hit the scene, a new trend in direct marketing emerged. Sending diskettes in the mail soon became extremely popular. A 3.5-inch diskette can hold approximately 1.44 megabytes of information. In the early days of computing, that was a lot of space and perfect for sending anything from text and graphics to software.

No company was better at using diskettes for marketing than America Online (AOL) in the early 1990s. In 1993 AOL began sending out more than 250 million diskettes to the mass market. The diskettes carried AOL software on them and could be found almost everywhere—in your mailbox, in your magazines, and at the nearest computer store. Within a year's time, the software diskettes garnered AOL one million subscribers. Why? Because by simply inserting a diskette into a computer, consumers could sample the AOL Internet access product for free.

Toward the middle of the decade, CD-ROM became popular as a marketing tool and still is today. CD-ROMs can store approximately 650 megabytes of data, or about 300,000 pages of text. Because of its large storage capacity, CD-ROMs are perfect for multimedia—audio, video, and rich graphics. They are relatively inexpensive to produce and they're light-weight and durable. It's not uncommon to request an evaluation CD from a company in order to "test-drive" new software. You can even "burn" (encode) your own CD-ROM at home for the cost of the equipment and supplies.

Electronic Mail

Electronic mail, or e-mail, has rapidly become a marketing technology that we now take for granted. E-mail is nothing more than text messages that are sent through a network to a specified individual or group. Many people use it as one of their primary means of communication with the outside world—it's fast, cheap, and fairly reliable. Messages can be sent instantaneously across thousands of miles to thousands of recipients. Nine out of ten times, I will send someone an e-mail message rather than pick up the phone to call.

Marketers have found several ways to use e-mail to reach potential customers and other target audiences. While highly useful, it can be a useful tool. It can also be a dangerous tool when companies use it to "spam" consumers. Spamming is the twentieth-century art of mass mailing unwanted e-mail messages to thousands of unsuspecting computer users. To many people, nothing is more annoying than finding an unsolicited e-mail advertisement in your e-mailbox. The general public has cried out against spamming, and several organizations, services, and vehicles now "fry" (attempt to eliminate) spam. Legislation that could prohibit the practice is also in the works.

Websites

As the Internet and the World Wide Web began gaining popularity, so did new ways to market using websites. Suddenly companies were putting their universal resource locators (URLs) on everything. These so-called Web addresses have become common fixtures on letterhead, business cards, brochures, and marketing give-aways. They can also be found in print ads, on radio and television, and even on the backs of shirts. The goal is to get consumers to visit your site and ultimately to have them click on advertisements and actually buy something. Electronic commerce, or e-commerce, had arrived. The advent of permission-based marketing—the practice of obtaining a person's permission to communicate with them and provide advertising—made capturing a person's e-mail address one of the most important things you could do with a website, according to many online marketing professionals.

Banner Advertisements

In 1995 banner ads appeared on the online marketing scene. A banner is a small, rectangular-shaped ad with graphics and a link to a website. They have been called by several names, including electronic billboards. Today they are expected to do one of two things—either lead to an actual online sale or build a product or service's brand. They evolved from simple text messages in a box to ads with eye-catching animated pictures.

In mid-1996 the advertising model for banner ads changed. Instead of being charged by the number of visitors to a site, advertisers were beginning to be charged by the "click-through" rate. The click-through is nothing more than clicking on the banner ad and being transported to the advertiser's site. For the companies that offered banner ad hosting, the accountability level rose substantially. They were accountable for the number of visitors they generated and for the quality of those prospects.

With the increasing number of websites and the highly competitive content available, banner ads started to lose their effectiveness. Click-through rates dropped dramatically, and Internet advertisers began to search for new and more effective ways to reach online consumers. The online advertising industry was only in its infancy. In late 1999 Forrester Research predicted that global spending for online advertising will reach $33 billion by 2004, one-third of which will be spent outside of the United States.

◆ PUBLIC RELATIONS

Since the first days of public relations in the seventeenth century, the goal of the profession has always been to build relationships, increase communication, and influence perceptions and behavior of either a broad audience or a targeted one. Until the late twentieth century, the strategies and techniques that public relations practitioners used did not waver much. Throughout this time period, practitioners used press releases, special events, and in-person meetings to accomplish their goals of influencing the general public and obtaining coverage by the news media. They still do today, in fact. Significant change didn't occur until the mid-1990s when technology made communication easier and much more immediate.

The tools of public relations today are similar to those used by marketing professionals—diskettes, CD-ROM, the Internet, websites, and e-mail all play key roles in how public relations people get their messages across. It's common today for a journalist to receive a press kit with either a diskette or a CD-ROM included. Companies hope that journalists will use these tools to experience their products first-hand, or perhaps to better educate themselves about the company and its customers.

Websites have become instrumental in helping journalists with their research efforts. They can visit a site, review company and product information, watch a video, and gather contact information. But traditional press kits are rapidly becoming a waste of money and paper because today's technology-savvy journalists know that most information can be found online.

E-mail has also become an effective tool for public relations practitioners to reach journalists to secure news coverage. It's cheap and interactive. Responses to e-mail inquiries can be sent within a few seconds of receiving the original request for information. Many journalists actually prefer to be contacted via e-mail because it saves them critical time, especially when they're on deadline.

Reality Check

The object of most public relations campaigns today is to get free publicity. Public relations industry professionals spend a lot of time discussing how to develop strategy, shape reputations, influence perceptions, and build brands, but most senior-level executives will admit that they most desire the free press. For many people, "getting ink" (having the company's name published) is their unspoken primary goal. To them, press coverage can accomplish many things, even some of the previously mentioned objectives. Today, this type of free publicity is critical to building a company or product's brand. If the publicity incorporates a company's key messages, then it can also help build a reputation or influence the target audience's perceptions. Sometimes, it can even help to move the stock price.

Similar to technology, the ability to obtain press coverage has also evolved over the last century. For the most part, the publications and broadcast outlets that tied editorial coverage to a company's willingness to pay for advertising have disappeared. A few holdouts, however, still offer news coverage only if you purchase advertising or agree to buy reprinted articles from them. I have also been in a situation where my company was promised inclusion in a magazine or book "without any financial obligation on your part" only to receive a bill later.

Television News Scams

One of the biggest "editorial" scams I saw in the late 1990s involved broadcast programs. These programs tried to take advantage of the increased interest in high-tech and business news. They also tried to take advantage of budding high-tech companies that, perhaps, were not as news savvy as they should have been. Over the course of about a year and a half, I built a list of more than a dozen business and trade television shows that featured prominent hosts, such as Casper Weinberger or Mark Hamill (of *Star Wars* fame). They would build so-called news programming around hot new technologies or business trends that would capture the general public's interest. They promoted these shows as excellent vehicles, not only for widespread news coverage of products, services, and trends, but also as a good way to position companies as industry leaders.

Here's how it worked: An assistant to the producer would call a CEO and say that the show was considering the company for inclusion in a segment on a particular branch of the industry. The assistant wanted to talk in-depth with the CEO to gather research, and "if" the company were selected, it would be featured and broadcast on CNBC.

I was always the lucky one to call these assistants back. The first question I would ask, having been a television reporter for more than a decade, was if any costs were associated with the opportunity. That question generally caused a lot of hemming and hawing. It would always turn out that, yes, there were some "marketing" costs to the tune of about $45,000. Now, I realize I am generalizing these programs, but the cost was always between $25,000 and $50,000.

These costs, I was told, would pay for the production of the segment as well as an integrated marketing campaign, including exposure on the World Wide Web. As part of the deal, a company would receive a copy of the three- to five-minute video segment, which it could use for promotional purposes. As for when and where it would air on CNBC, it was generally shown on Monday mornings at 9 a.m. on cable channels that carried *some* CNBC programming; it was not a part of actual CNBC programming. Furthermore, if you looked at the cable channels that aired the show, they were in markets such as Billings, Montana, and Boulder, Colorado.

They were not in the top-50 television markets in the United States nor were they considered the business or high-tech hubs of America.

I was surprised by the number of these shows and the high-caliber people in the public eye who lent their names to them. I was really shocked by the number of companies that actually paid for these opportunities. News is free. Remember that. You don't have to pay tens of thousands of dollars to get news coverage.

More News, More News Opportunities

In the late 1990s publications began to get extremely specialized. For example, in the high-tech arena, magazines were dedicated to personal computers (PCs), Macintosh computers, networks, the Internet, mobile computing, Java, Yahoo!, high-tech–related business, computer shopping, and computer reselling.

Computer television shows sprang up as well. C/net Central was complementary to its online website. ZDTV created its own 24-hour computer network. CNN had a computer show and a high-tech unit out of San Francisco, and at least a half-dozen local or syndicated computer or Internet-related broadcasts debuted. Unfortunately, by the end of the 1990s, only a few programs managed to stay on the air, and ZDTV was having a hard time finding a home with cable companies across the country. By the end of 1999, ZDTV was still not available in the San Francisco Bay area where it originated. It was not available in the one place where high-tech activity thrived most—Silicon Valley.

See and Be Seen—Tradeshows

Not only were many computer and Internet-related news opportunities available, but it also seemed that the end of the twentieth century brought its share of industry trade shows and conferences. These amazing shows consisted of huge convention centers filled with companies demonstrating and pitching their wares. I started working the tradeshow floors in 1996. It seemed to me at that time that more people were working the booths than were attending the events. And then it got worse.

It also seemed that the people who attended cared more about the free give-aways than about gathering information about products, services, and business solutions. A perfect example of this phenomenon was at a Customer Relationship Management show in Washington, D.C., in the spring of 1999. The show was slow. There was little traffic, and no one seemed to be coming to our booth. For half a day, we watched another company across from us continually fill every seat in their small makeshift auditorium. What were they doing that we weren't? We finally realized that they were giving away free stuff. So, we put our give-away t-shirts on the chairs in our makeshift auditorium and filled every seat, every time. It was pitiful. The leads we generated were useless, but we had reached our quota.

As I attended more tradeshows, I began to see that they never got the traffic that had been promised. I think the problem was that too many tradeshows and conferences began to meld into one another. There were no longer compelling reasons to attend. The big-name trade journalists didn't even bother to attend much anymore, so significant press opportunities dried up as well.

TWENTIETH-CENTURY TRENDS

One of the most fascinating trends of the last century involved a technology tool of the past and one of the future— television and computers. In July 1999 Nielsen Media Research conducted a study for AOL. It analyzed the television-viewing habits of American households that also owned computers and had Internet access. The study found that television viewing in Internet households—no matter how long households had been online—was significantly less than in non-online households. This was actually the third consecutive year that these two organizations conducted this study. The findings turned out to be statistically consistent to those released by AOL and Nielsen in January 1997 and August 1998, even though they found that Internet use had penetrated deeper into the mass market.

Another survey, by Media Metrix, found that more than one-half of all households with PCs (52 percent or 19 million households) now had a television set and computer in the same room. In addition, simultaneous use of TV sets and PCs located in the same room has grown from 16.4 million households to 18.1 million households in a period of about six months. Media Metrix analysts theorize that one hand may hold the remote control while the other balances family finances, checks e-mail, or surfs the Web between television programs. I can validate this theory because I do these things while sitting in a comfortable overstuffed chair with my laptop computer and wireless modem.

Radio

Since the early 1900s, listening to the radio has been an extremely popular pastime. People love to listen to it in their cars, homes, and offices. Some take the radio with them when they go to a park, a beach, or even the gym. Today, they no longer actually need a radio—they have the computer.

Radio stations across the United States are now extending their reach onto the Web and are capitalizing on one of their most valuable resources—their signal—to draw consumers to their websites. According to an Arbitron New Media study, 13% of Americans have listened to the radio online. The study is also significant because it reveals that 51% of the people who have listened to radio online tune into their local stations. OnRadio, the largest network of information and entertainment portals on the Internet, has more than 40 affiliate stations that are streaming their signals to produce an overall listening audience of more than 20 million people. In terms of building brand, this activity is a great benefit because radio stations have the ability to reach a worldwide audience. It also helps the stations open up a whole new revenue stream.

Webcasting, as it's called, offers great promise for the future because it could change how people buy and respond to music. Research has found that Webcast audiences aren't just listening to their favorite programs; they are interacting with online information and advertising in surprising numbers. According to the Arbitron New Media/Northstar's Interactive Study of Webcast audiences, Webcasts trigger significant interaction—almost 70 percent of online listeners click for content information and almost 60 percent click through for advertiser information, while tuned to streaming media programming. Almost one-half of the Webcast audience clicks on online ads at the site, and almost one-half of those people actually buy the advertised products.

News

As the twentieth century drew to a close, most media outlets—print and broadcast—were scrambling to create an online presence. Most magazines, newspapers, and radio and television stations today have created complementary websites where their audiences can go to find a lot of the same information that is available in traditional form as well as enhanced or additional information. Stories on the Web are generally more detailed because the number of column inches or a producer's stopwatch does not limit journalists. Many general news websites also offer continuously updated information, such as stock quotes, sports scores, and weather.

At the time this convergence of traditional and Web news was taking place, two distinct trends were evolving. The first trend involved print magazines. The philosophy surrounding which news media—print or Web—was more important was definitely changing. The editor-in-chief of a popular computer magazine told PR Newswire that she encouraged her staff to think of their publication as a daily Web newspaper that just happened to create a wonderful print edition. It used to be the other way around.

The second trend fell along those lines as well. Three popular high-tech industry trade publications actually shut down their traditional print operations at the end of 1999 in order to concentrate solely on their electronic versions. *Byte* magazine ended its run in March but reemerged online a few months later and *Windows* magazine closed down in August with plans to be strictly electronic. The reasons behind these decisions were strictly business-focused. Advertising revenues were starting to decline, and some publishing houses believed that the print market would not support rapid growth like the Web would and could.

For journalists, reporting online gave them more freedom to expand their stories and to be featured as regular columnists. For some, deadlines were still a part of their daily lives, but others achieved more flexibility because they didn't have to fill physical space or broadcast minutes. Breaking news was truly breaking news. It happened, they wrote about it, and it was posted.

Extranets

One trend that also began in the late 1990s and that has picked up momentum involves extranets. Extranets are secure intranets that can be accessed from trusted external parties, such as customers, consultants, resellers, business suppliers, financial partners, and various other people who don't officially work for your organization yet use your resources. According to Forrester Research, more than one-half of the Fortune 1000 are using extranets today. Forrester predicts that of the companies not currently deploying extranets, more than 80 percent are planning to offer them within the next two years. So far we have seen extranet activity picked up by those in the banking, technology, consumer packaged goods, and telecommunications industries.

Extranets offer companies a cost-effective way to improve communications and ultimately increase their bottom lines. Instead of having the appropriate party dial into a pro-prietary information system, they could easily access the information via a secure website. Imagine an extranet that could be accessed by customers and clients who were in search of product and software updates, new product releases, delivery information, and order statuses. Resellers could visit a company's extranet to get the latest price lists, product update news, marketing collateral, and other infor-mation that was crucial to their success. Partners could access an extranet to learn about and track the progress of new products and services, company mergers and acqui-sitions, and mutually beneficial customer wins. Extranets give customers, partners, resellers, and suppliers an easy way to stay informed. And they give the host company a cost-effective way to increase communications with those who can impact their bottom lines.

THE INTERNET— A FORCE TO BE DEALT WITH IN THE NEW MILLENNIUM

As the twentieth century drew to a close, the word *Internet* became ingrained in our daily language, and for many people became a part of our daily activities. When talking about the Internet, however, it's important to understand that the Internet and the World Wide Web are two distinct entities. The Internet is a collection of networks that provide robust, multiple paths for all data traffic. The World Wide Web is the premier information-retrieval application that happens to run on top of the Internet. Both provide great value to those involved in marketing and publicity.

WHAT IS THE INTERNET?

The Internet actually got its start in the late 1960s. The Defense Advanced Research Projects Agency (DARPA) was the parent of the ARPANet, which was designed to link military bases, governmental research facilities, and research universities that were working on military projects. In 1983 ARPANet was split into two networks, one for the military and one for research. By 1985 The National Science Foundation (NSF) had taken over ARPANet, which was by then reaching all supercomputers. In 1990, the first commercial provider of Internet dial-up access came on-line and the Internet started taking on the form we now know today.

THE WORLD WIDE WEB

The World Wide Web is a graphical interface for the Internet that consists of Internet services that provide access to documents, which, in turn, provide hyperlinks to other documents, multimedia files and sites. These links are graphics or different-colored text that contain programming code that provide the actual connection to another site.

The Internet and the World Wide Web have become part of everyday life for many people. Today's statistics prove it: the average number of minutes spent online each day is about 47, and the number of hours spent each week is about 5.5. An online research firm, eStats, estimates that 94% of people accessing the Web do so at least partially to send and receive e-mail messages. Other reasons for being online include gathering news and information, researching data, participating in chat rooms, posting to bulletin boards, playing games, and shopping.

EVOLUTION OF THE WEB PAGE: A TRIP TO THE GROCERY STORE

First Came Presence

In the beginning there was electronic messaging or e-mail. E-mail was developed before the Internet was available to send electronic messages within a closed network. With the advent of the Internet, which could send and receive packets of information over Internet protocol (IP), a whole new way of presenting and communicating information was born.

The Web page became the new billboard advertisement for institutions, businesses, and individuals—for basically anyone who wanted to say "hello world" on the information highway. This first generation of the website was very simple. It included only the basics—the company name, address, phone number, and some company or product information. The home page could almost be referred to as an electronic welcome mat or a new form of electronic yellow pages that included an advertisement. The purpose of the page was to send a message to visitors that said "if you need any more information, then pick up the telephone and give us a call." At that point, most people did not have e-mail accounts or understand the concept of e-mail, so e-mail addresses were not included.

The website as a method of communication was primarily a one-way street. Companies broadcasted their information via their website but did not ask for any information back. This first-generation site enhanced the marketing capability of businesses by having a worldwide audience and presence, but it was not interactive.

Let's Integrate, "Can We Talk?"

Businesses and individuals who were savvy to the capabilities of the World Wide Web quickly blazed ahead to the second generation of Web pages, which gave customers and prospects access to a wealth of information. As part of the second generation of websites, in-depth information, such as online catalogs, began to appear. Consumers were also able to interact with the website and had the ability to send questions. Bilateral communication, or the ability to send and receive information via the Web, had arrived.

One of the first large organizations to realize the interactive capabilities of the Web was FedEx (www.fedex.com). The FedEx site provided a gateway to information in which a visitor could type in the tracking number of a shipment and get back a response from the FedEx shipping database. FedEx saved millions of dollars in its tracking call center operations and provided a new service to its customers.

With this new capability, information was no longer static; it was dynamic, meaning created "on the fly" and presented back out to the desktop Web browser. Feedback forms that let people input their customer information, update the company databases, and pass on recommendations for improvement were introduced in the second generation.

In order to grant this type of customer access to information, security software and hardware was developed to protect the companies from unfriendly hacking into the internal systems. Ordering systems were starting to be developed. Ordering a product or service over the Web at this point had been done either via e-mail, online forms, or partly over the phone. Certified security systems were just being developed to protect sensitive information, such as credit card numbers over the IP. Not only were companies offering product and service information, but they were also developing ways of collecting information such as the number of Web pages that were visited and the likes and dislikes of their customers.

Enable Me. Can I Give You My Credit Card?

The third generation of the Web page entered into the e-commerce stage of development. Systems were developed to securely encrypt information from the Web browser to companies' Web servers. Now, secure transactions could take place in which credit card information could be safely transferred, and access to internal systems, such as account information, could be verified. New business processes were being developed for e-commerce. Companies such as Amazon.com (www.amazon.com) were implementing business models to sell books exclusively via the Web. They started gathering not only the credit card numbers but also information about the buying habits of their customers.

Amazon.com used this easy yet sophisticated customer intelligence to reach a new level of interactivity with customers. As a result, Amazon.com was able to produce intelligent, computer-generated recommendations on books based on which previous purchases were made and increased its sales and revenue as a result. Amazon.com customers could now do their own purchasing, type in their own shipping and credit card information, and avoid interacting with a live human being throughout the experience if they so chose.

These new business-to-consumer and business-to-business capabilities were now quickly being built into websites. On the business-to-business side, suppliers could access information important to them via the Web. Extranets were also developed and provided an online experience in which organizations that depended on each other's products and services could exchange information securely.

Where Do We Go From Here, and How About Some Groceries?

For many companies and organizations, the website has evolved into a virtual storefront on the main street of the World Wide Web. To use a grocery store analogy, when we all moved into a new neighborhood, no one knew where to buy groceries or how to get there. We stopped by the first place we saw as we cruised the streets or we looked in the telephone book's yellow pages. When we entered the store, we didn't know anyone who worked there, so we fumbled around, trying to find exactly what we wanted. It was frustrating and we had to wait in a line in order to finally purchase the groceries.

A sophisticated website can be like a consumer-friendly grocery store, only better. A good website is organized so you can get exactly what you need, efficiently and without being frustrated in the process. It has great features and takes a convenient, sensible approach to where the Webmaster puts the items you want. It offers quick access, quality products, and a place to ask questions and receive prompt responses.

You, the consumer, build a relationship with the "store." It knows you by name, knows what you like to buy, lets you know when your items are on sale, gives you coupons, and keeps your "rewards" card on file. The store (website) is stocked with new items. Its intelligent systems know, without asking, if you want paper or plastic. After becoming more familiar with the neighborhood (the World Wide Web), you find other grocery stores (websites) that better meet your needs.

Where Do You Live? Tips for Website Success

I have to mention a practice that I find quite ironic when thinking about the evolution of websites. In the first-generation websites, visitors found only the basics—the phone number and address of the business. Contact information was the primary message. The majority of today's websites have unwittingly eliminated the basics. How many times have you spent five to ten minutes navigating through a site, trying to find a contact person's name, the company's phone number or address, or something other than an impersonal e-mail address? Many businesses today have forgotten that a website is a communications vehicle.

Believe it or not, it is sometimes necessary to speak to a live person or to send the company something via traditional mail service. Just the other day, I searched on a prominent bank's website, frantically trying to find any kind of contact information for a public relations person. It was nowhere to be found. I finally had to use the Webmaster feedback e-mail address to ask if such a person existed. The site had a public relations page for journalists, which included press releases and other media materials. You would have thought that the public relations person's name and contact information would be listed somewhere on that page or at least attached to a press release, but it wasn't. I wasted far too much time trying to find this information.

- Be strategic about where you place the basic contact information. Do not bury it. Visitors should not have to access page after page of information trying to find it.

- Always include the company's address and main tele-phone number as well as fax number and number and main e-mail address. It's also good to include a toll-free phone number if you have one.

- Always include easy-to-find sales, marketing, and public relations contact information. Keep this current so visitors don't waste their time (and yours) talking to the wrong person. Remember not to bury this important business information somewhere deep within or off the Web page.

- If you really want to be proactive and ultimately success-ful, place the basic contact information on every page of the website.

THE NEED FOR SPEED

When I go to work, my computer connection is as fast as lightning. My company has all of its employees hooked up to a network that has a T1 line straight to the Internet. A T-carrier system is a high-speed pipe that uses excess capacity from traditional phone companies. Its raw data rate is 1.544 megabits per second. It's fast, although not fast enough to support TV-quality, full-motion video. When I surf the Net, the Web pages I choose—no matter how sophisticated or full of complicated graphics—are usually downloaded quickly. I have become spoiled with the fast network connection.

At home, it's another story. I use a wireless modem with an average speed of 19.2 kilobits per second, and it feels as slow as molasses. Web pages take forever to download. If someone were to send me a PowerPoint presentation via e-mail, I would be out of commission for a long time—perhaps hours.

I will go out on a limb and generalize that my home expe-rience is probably pretty common, except in the nation's silicon valleys, alleys, and corridors. Granted, research has shown that more than one million North American households already enjoy broadband (high-speed data trans-mission) access to the Internet and that the number is expected to reach almost 26 million people by 2003. I would guess, however, that the rest of the population probably has a traditional phone line modem that sends and receives data at between 28.8 and 56 kilobits per second. I would also guess that those who have lightning-fast connections at work are pretty frustrated at home—just like me.

No one questions that the need for speed is definite and immediate—not only to enhance the computer user experience but also to be successful with tomorrow's marketing and online advertising efforts. Marketers, ad agencies, and website developers have expanded their creativity to include rich graphics, snazzy videos, streaming media, and all sorts of other bells and whistles and tools and techniques that can capture and hold an audience's attention. The question is how long they will have to wait until the majority of the American public has a super-fast connection.

The Eight-Second Rule

There has been a lot of talk about just how much time a company actually has to capture and captivate online consumers. The truth is scary. Zona Research conducted a study that found that one-third of online shoppers waiting for Web pages to download will give up after only eight seconds. Zone Research predicted that in 1999, this failure to wait could cost Web merchants as much as $4.35 billion in lost e-commerce sales.

In Zona's report, "The Need for Speed," it stated that in 1999, 44.1 million people in the United States were online shoppers and that another 37.5 million of the population intended to follow suit. Further research by Zona revealed that more than one-third of Web users may simply give up trying to buy an item over the Internet when frustrated with an online shopping experience. Zona Research estimated that users' frustrations could result in as much as $4.35 billion in U.S. e-commerce sales being at risk each year solely because of unacceptable download times.

How Fast is Fast and How Soon Will it be Available?

Several high-speed options are available right now for the general public. I must first warn you that they're more expensive than a traditional phone line connection. Right now, it's a question of supply; the demand is there. Not all of these technologies are available everywhere.

The most common high-speed connection is called *integrated services digital network* (ISDN), which can be secured from the telephone company. ISDN provides data speeds of up to 128 kilobits per second. Connecting to an ISDN line requires a network terminal and an ISDN adapter. Most telephone companies offer ISDN, but it may not be the most cost-effective option.

Cable modems that use your cable TV connection instead of a phone line to connect to the Internet are another high-speed option. Because the bandwidth of coaxial cable is much higher than that of the standard phone line your telephone company uses, the speed advantage of cable modems versus regular phone modems is profound. Cable modem speeds range from 500 kilobits per second to 10 megabits per second. Cable modems have two disadvantages, though. First, the fast speeds are only for downloading of files and information. The upload is much slower because the cable TV network was originally meant as a delivery system into the home. Cable modem systems are going to have to find a way to provide high speed in both directions in order to successfully compete with the telephone companies. The second disadvantage is that cable is a shared resource. If everyone on your block signs up for cable modem service and downloads large files at the same time, then everybody's speed drops.

Some communities around the country have access to digital subscriber lines (DSLs), which can provide an equally high-speed connection over a regular phone line. An HDSL line can provide speeds of up to 1.544 megabits per second. The advantage DSL has over cable modems is that this technology provides lightning-fast downloads and uploads, which translates into a lot less frustration for impatient Web surfers like me. A whole family of *digital telecommunications protocols,* collectively known as xDSL, were designed to allow high-speed data communication over the existing copper telephone lines between end users and telephone companies.

Satellite high-speed data services are also on tap for the coming decade. Satellites are capable of delivering data at speeds of up to 45 megabits per second, which is approximately 30 times faster than a T1 line, but in order to be successful with consumers, they'll have to offer two-way capability. Companies such as Lockheed, Teledisic, and Hughes Network Systems all hope to provide these high-speed connections.

Trials are also underway that offer high-speed fiberoptic cable straight to the curbside (also called *fiber to the home*). Companies hoping to provide this high-speed service claim network access rates of up to 100 megabits per second, which is more than 1,700 times the speed of the fastest dial-up modem. A company called Media Fusion is developing technology it says can send data, voice, or video signals over electric power lines at speeds we can't even imagine—well over 2.5 gigabits per second. In summary, the good news is that speeds will continue their inexorable increase in the future. That means you will be able to participate in a high-quality, real-time videoconference or easily watch a movie downloaded from the Web in the not-too-distant future.

These emerging communications methods greatly reduce the bandwidth constraints of the twentieth century and promise a much more sophisticated online advertising industry in the future. Unfortunately, the rollouts are always slower than customers want, and the coverage is generally spotty. Some industry analysts say it could take up to seven years or more before some of these technologies are widely available.

Broadband

In the coming years, we'll continue to hear a lot about broadband. Broadband is the generic term for a transmission medium capable of supporting a wide range of frequencies, typically from audio up to video frequencies. Today the term often describes high-speed data transmissions, such as the ones previously mentioned, that are sufficient enough to carry live video-on-demand over the Internet.

In addition to faster and easier access to websites, broadband offers always-on connections and more bandwidth for applications. Broadband will be the key to new applications and content-rich services. With DSL, online banking and investment services are already taking advantage of the always-on capability. They provide a steady stream of information to consumers, such as account updates, breaking financial news, and large educational documents. With high-speed capabilities, consumers have access to enticing sales videos, demos, and product samples that once were too cumbersome and time-consuming to download. Companies in the entertainment industry are delivering a wealth of content through broadband portal sites featuring interactive games and video advertising. Virtual reality and video e-mail also benefit from the data-carrying capacity of broadband technology.

Broadband advertising is being touted as the "next big thing" in the online advertising industry and has a good chance to become a large segment of the online ad market. According to a November 1998 report by market research firm Jupiter Communications, one-third of all online ads will be rich media by 2002. With new interactive features and specific targeted demographics, high-speed service providers will have the goods to warrant even higher advertising rates.

CASE STUDY: REDEFINING INTERACTIVITY

Ten years ago, proponents of interactive television promised to simultaneously entertain audiences, advertise products, and incorporate a point of purchase—all in a seamless viewing experience. Today, the technologies to deliver these promises are rapidly maturing. But the medium will be broadband, not broadcast. According to a report from Forrester Research, broadband will redefine interactivity by delivering a continuous stream of engaging, information-rich entertainment that stimulates participation.

Broadband's coming-out party is already underway, and the tools and interfaces to deliver immersing interactivity—an environment featuring visual imagery, audio accompaniment, and participatory interaction via an invisible interface—are starting to hit the market. With a rapidly growing audience and the technology in place, Forrester expects that thousands of addictive broadband experiences will be available on portals and entertainment sites within five years.

Today's limited resource pool of creative talent is the biggest challenge to making the broadband experience a reality. Forrester believes that the necessary talent will emerge in three phases, starting with the first breakthrough experiences from a few small broadband boutiques. These early interactive episodes—shot direct to digital on shoestring budgets—will expose broadband's potential as a truly new medium.

Fearful of losing their audience to the Internet, major media companies will launch their own broadband initiatives while interactive ad agencies such as Razorfish will create hothouses for new talent development. By 2003, the flow of money and opportunity will produce a burgeoning market for entertainment architects, similar to the Web developers that arose in 1996. These shops will team with deep-pocketed content providers looking to buy rather than build sophisticated interactivity.

Although users will not tolerate distracting banner ads, Forrester believes that the early backing for broadband content will come from advertisers. Because audiences are "locked in" to an experience, ads and promotions subtly woven into the storyline will naturally drive viewers to action. Early broadband efforts will blur the distinction between entertainment and product promotion, with product appearances serving as a link to deeper brand-specific experiences. These activities will evolve into enviromercials that immerse users in brand experiences and interactive selling environments that greatly expand the information available to buyers.

With the emergence of talent and backing, content development will move from occasional projects to year-round production for a rapidly expanding audience. By 2003, broadband experiences will become commonplace as everyone from sports teams to media giants offers increasingly more content.

(Courtesy: Forrester Research)

EFFECTIVE MARKETING ON THE WEB

One of the most important things a company can do to ensure its success in today's business world is to rethink the traditional mix of marketing opportunities and find innovative ways to integrate new technologies and techniques into their programs. I recommend taking advantage of the World Wide Web to the fullest.

◆ RESEARCH ON THE WEB

Throughout my career, I have tried to provide intelligent counsel about the marketing and publicity programs that I propose to my employers, clients, and fellow practitioners. A large part of that intelligence comes from research. Research is an invaluable tool that can be used to learn more about target audiences, market issues and trends, and programs that have a history of success or failure. The World Wide Web has become a wonderful source of research material that can be used for marketing and publicity purposes. You only have to know how to get to a search engine in order to find the information you seek.

Today, you no longer have to memorize the URLs of the companies or products for which you are looking. You simply type in a topic or the company name, and the search engine does the work for you. The end result is that you receive several options on your screen. You pick the one that seems closest to what you are looking for. Finally, with the click of a mouse, you can find websites, message boards, news articles, press releases, marketing collateral, audio and video clips, databases, photographs, and graphics.

Message Boards and Newsgroups

Message boards and newgroups have become useful sources of information for research on marketing and corporate communications. Message boards and newsgroups enable marketers to eavesdrop on customers, investors, and other interested parties. They can easily learn what people think about their products and services, or about the company in general. If comments start to become negative and grow in number and consistency, then you can become proactive with your crisis communications plans. Online watchdogs, such as eWatch, specialize in monitoring these Internet conversations for a fee. They use key words to pick up all online messages about your company or product and provide you with a tracking report.

Message boards and newsgroups are wonderful sources for monitoring your company's reputation or public persona. When I was investigating new career opportunities, the first place I went to for my research was the company's investor message board. I found many companies that had investors complaining about poor management, lack of cash, large employee turnover, loss of intellectual knowledge, and so forth. It was a great place to quickly identify warning signs about a particular company. Red flags about products and services also tend to pop up on these boards. Marketing and public relations professionals within the organization can learn a lot about perceptions from these messages and take action if necessary.

I also find these communications channels invaluable for identifying new trends and monitoring the competition. When I worked for Metricom, a wireless modem company, the savvy investors had great insight into the future of wireless Internet communications and often predicted consumer trends—good and bad. Later, when I joined BackWeb Technologies, I often went to our competitors' investor message boards to see if our name popped up. Sure enough, one day I found a message from a manager of an industry-leading behemoth of a corporation who was bad-mouthing my company. The worst part was that he had no accurate or personal knowledge of what my company did, or that we were actually providing products and services to his company. Because he identified himself in the message, we were able to talk with his supervisors and ensure that he didn't do any further damage. I wonder if that gentleman is still with his company

◆ VIDEO ON THE WEB

Before we can discuss the role of video (or even rich graphics) in tomorrow's marketing and publicity activities, we must revisit the need for speed and bandwidth. Most businesses have some sort of high-speed pipeline to the Internet and the outside world. For some, it is an ISDN line, which is a digital phone line that offers faster speeds than traditional phone line modems—up to 128 kilobits per second. Other companies use T1 lines that offer speeds of up to 1.544 Megabits per second. DSLs and cable Internet access will soon be broadly available. As a result, the general consumer will have extremely high-speed connections at home. All of these Internet access options enable fast downloads of Web pages and the delivery of rich audio, video, and graphics. Simple text delivery is extremely fast.

Many companies around the world are taking advantage of this high-speed, high-bandwidth capability through their use of video. With the popularity of the Internet, they are now creating inexpensive online marketing tools such as video testimonials by customers, heart-felt video messages from the CEO, close-up and personal demonstrations of products, highlights of speeches and industry presentations, and eye-catching, attention-grabbing movies that help build brand and corporate image.

Streaming Media

Streaming audio and video over the Internet have become a huge part of online marketing. The term streaming refers to audio (sound) and video (pictures) that are transferred over a network and play as the content is still being downloaded. In the past, you had to wait a long time for a large audio or video file to completely download onto your computer before you could play it. With today's streaming capabilities, you may have to wait a few seconds for the first part of the audio or video to download, but then you can begin listening or watching as it continues to download in the background. This technology gives users an experience similar to that of watching television or listening to the radio.

The most common format for streaming audio and video belongs to RealNetworks. The company develops and markets software products and services designed to enable users of personal computers and other consumer electronic devices to send and receive audio, video, and other mul-timedia services using the Web. In most cases, you (the marketer) need to have special streaming server software on your Web server, and your Web visitors need to have the right plug-in. With the capabilities of streaming media, we are seeing a dramatic increase in both the amount and quality of creative content produced exclusively for the Web.

RealNetworks' RealSystem software is used to deliver content on more than 85% of all streaming media–enabled Web pages. Every week, more than 145,000 hours of live sports, music, news, and entertainment are broadcast over the Internet using RealSystem technology. Hundreds of thousands of hours of content are also available on-demand. The RealNetworks family of websites is among the top audio/video destinations on the Web and ranks consistently in the top-25 most popular sites on the Internet.

If you visit www.realguide.real.com, you will find thousands of websites that allow you to watch or listen to television news, tune into your favorite radio station, or experience live concerts, sporting events, and religious programming. You can even preview the latest music, videos, movie trailers, and MP3s. (MP3 is short for MPEG Audio Layer 3, which can compress one minute of music onto one megabyte of disk space to provide compact disc–quality sound.) The majority of these outlets are using streaming media to help increase their brand equity.

CASE STUDY: STREAMING HELPS IMPROVE BRAND AWARENESS

A 1999 study by Millward Brown Interactive indicated that streaming media advertising significantly increases ad recognition, brand awareness, and brand perception. The study evaluated streaming media advertising from 800.COM, an online consumer electronics retailer and a RealNetworks advertising customer.

In this study, 800.COM tested the brand impact of its streaming media advertising using a rigorous research methodology for evaluating advertising effectiveness. Results of the study showed that recall of the 800.COM brand increased significantly after a single additional streaming advertising exposure. Fifty percent of the people who were exposed to 800.COM's streaming ad noticed and remembered it in connection with the brand. This recognition represented a 213 percent increase over people who were not exposed to the ad. Additionally, the number of people in the test group who were aware of 800.COM's brand after being exposed to the streaming media ad was 160 percent greater than the number of people in the control group who were aware of the 800.COM brand.

The considerable jump in 800.COM's branding metrics indicated that streaming media advertising is a significant online brand-building vehicle. The study also showed that streaming media advertising had a positive impact on brand perception, including perceptions of 800.COM's popularity, competitive differentiation, and value proposition. In addition to exceptional branding impact, 800.COM's streaming media ads had superior click-through rates compared to other forms of online advertising that 800.COM was running.

(Courtesy: RealNetworks)

◆ PORTALS

Toward the end of 1999, a lot of media attention was focused on portals, especially by the computer and Internet trade press. Some people called it just another hyped technology, like Push in 1997, but many felt confident that portals were here to stay. A portal is basically a website that serves as a window to the rest of the World Wide Web. Its purpose is to guide Web surfers to just about anything they want to find online and provide as many services as possible in one place, such as free e-mail accounts, stock listings, and personalized news. It can be a computer user's one-stop destination for news and information once connected to the Internet.

From a marketing and advertising perspective, the first goal of a portal is to capture and lock in customer "eyeballs" and obtain valuable information, such as e-mail addresses. Portals allow people to interact with content (advertising especially), so it's in the portals' best interest to keep the audience once they've arrived. The ultimate goal of a portal is to generate advertising revenue. It's been said that the most lucrative websites on the Internet will be those that people use as their "start page"—the first page that appears when they achieve a connection.

Another trend that began appearing in late 1999 revolved around vertical portals—a portal website with tightly focused content designed for a particular audience. Garden.com (www.garden.com) is a portal site for gardening information. It touts itself as a "multi-dimensional garden resource that's interactive, innovative, and informative—the perfect site for home gardeners." You can ask gardening questions of its garden doctor; design your own garden with its onsite garden planner; buy seeds, plants, and tools in its online shopping area; and read about current gardening trends in garden.com magazine. You can even chat with other gardeners 24 hours a day. "Garden.com brings together the best of what the gardening world has to offer, from all around the world," so says its website messaging.

You may, one day, find a portal designed especially for marketers that provides you with great content. Although the content is already available today from a variety of locations, the value to you is that you don't have to go hunting for it.

What's in store for the future of portals? Many industry experts predict that only a few powerful consumer portals will be available from companies such as Yahoo!, Microsoft, and AOL. Others believe that technology will play a greater role in helping you sort through the content you desire. For example, there may be more reasoning and learning capability built into the delivery of portal content to you.

The big challenge for portals will be to make the experience more useful for the audience. In order to keep "eyeballs" on a portal, Web technology will become even more one-to-one and personalized. "The amount of information that is available on the Web is staggering, but the amount of intuition, energy, and smarts required to go find the things you need is also staggering," said Todd Johnson, vice president of worldwide marketing at BackWeb Technologies.

Johnson believes that portals will have to become much more dynamic and active. He suggests that your personalized portals could actually be different on different days. For example, you may want to see your stocks in the morning, during the trading day, and then when the market closes. Beyond that, you may want your screen space back for something else—perhaps the daily news or your weekly calendar. Portals will eventually have to become that intuitive in order to keep you as a loyal customer.

Finally, some say that it's possible that portal subscribers may have to pay for the experience one day. The reason is that the advertising model may not pay for the cost of aggregating all of the content that is relevant to you. And that could be the deciding factor as to the success and longevity of the portal.

INTERNET ADVERTISING

Despite cries that online ads don't work, spending for Internet advertising will continue to grow at a furious pace. Forrester Research estimates that global spending for online advertising will reach $33 billion by 2004. The increase in spending will come from several sources, including the reallocation of dollars from traditional media. Analysts predict that as the online audience continues to grow and e-commerce accelerates, more marketing dollars will be drawn to the Web. These trends will be enhanced by the arrival of new technologies that improve the accountability of Web advertising.

ONLINE SEMINARS

As access to the Internet and World Wide Web become ubiquitous, companies have the ability to market to a global audience at a relatively low cost. One of the more popular marketing techniques is to host online seminars, using the Internet, e-mail, and the telephone as the communications links. The end result is a live, interactive communications environment that delivers data, voice, and video through a standard browser.

I have found these online seminars and virtual meetings simple to attend. I have used a company called WebEx that offers a free service that promises to make Web-based meetings as productive as face-to-face meetings and as ubiquitous as e-mail. Its product is called WebEx Meeting Center and it requires only an ordinary browser and telephone. WebEx enables spontaneous sharing of documents, presentations, Web content, and applications.

I simply went to the site (www.webex.com) and registered as a new user. I was able to schedule a meeting and invite my target audience. WebEx sent automated meeting invitations, via e-mail, to the people I designated as invitees. I was assigned a meeting number, which was then given out to the people on my list. Anyone with the number could join the meeting. As part of this Web meeting system, I could chat with other participants by typing comments and responses in a little box near the bottom of the screen. It also offers the capability of sharing PowerPoint presentations, files of any size, and visits to websites.

For marketing and public relations purposes, I would recommend supplementing the e-mail invitation with other forms of advertising and promotion such as complementary direct mail and telemarketing. I would also recommend promoting online seminars on the company website.

Online seminars and meetings are cost-effective alternatives to traditionally uneventful conference calls. They're especially useful when your company or organization wants to share information about new products and services, demonstrate new software or Internet applications, inform shareholders about current financial information, or just provide supporting documentation. They're also good for briefing the news media when you have neither the time nor the money to go on an extensive press tour. Finally, you can communicate to any size audience.

CASE STUDY: WEBEX HOSTS WORLD'S-LARGEST INTERACTIVE MEETING

In July 1999, WebEx, the most popular meeting service on the Web, hosted the world's-largest Web-based meeting. More than 1,000 unique users logged on to WebEx's live Global Launch Event site to participate in the interactive meeting. The meeting was held to unveil the new WebEx Meeting Center services and to announce a substantial investment by Deutsche Telekom, Europe's largest telecommunications company.

"I was overwhelmed by the level of excitement and participation our Global Launch Event generated," said David Thompson, vice president of marketing at WebEx. "The enthusiasm around our WebEx Meeting Center is a sign of how businesses desperately need application services as feature-rich and scalable as WebEx."

(Courtesy: WebEx)

SEARCH ENGINES: GETTING VISITORS TO YOUR SITE

By now you probably have a website that your target audience can use to find information about your products or services or organization. However, you need to understand that a website is not a guarantee for instant business success. All too often the general public believes that having a Web presence means instant traffic and revenue. With more than 56,000,000 websites to choose from, though, how will your customers or your target audience find you?

This basic problem spawned a new online industry early in Internet development, which is the business of indexing Web page content and providing a method for computer users to search through a database of those pages for a particular keyword. If a match was found, then the user was provided a link to the website that contained the same keyword they had requested. The term *search engine* is used to describe a website that employs a software "engine" running in the background that continuously looks for websites to index. It also provides keyword information and links to related websites that it finds on request.

Search engines were an overnight success. Finally, users could find websites on the Internet that contained content in which they were interested. But finding only those sites that contained a specific word or phrase became yet another challenge. As businesses raced to bring their products and services online, the number of matches for keywords also increased. To improve this process, search engines began employing a ranking system. By ranking Web pages according to the number of times a keyword was used on the page or website, the search engine was able to return an ordered list to the person conducting the search. The websites that used the keyword several times would be ranked higher than those in which the keyword was mentioned fewer times.

If the Shoe Fits

A recent search on the AltaVista search engine for the keyword "shoes" finds 530,940 matches in its database. The website at the top of the list is www.williams-shoes.com. Those websites found at the bottom of the list are least likely to contain the information or products we want. As search engines mature, different ranking methods are being developed to help increase the probability that the websites found at the top of the ordered list are actually deserving of that position.

Get Me to the Top

Having your site appear in one of the top-ten positions on any particular search engine ranking can have a significant effect on the success of your online business. Using our previous example, why would you want to look at one of the websites listed at the bottom of the list when the site listed at the top is most likely to contain the shoes or information for which you are looking?

With more than 500 search engines to choose from, where should you start? The truth is that only a few of the search engines account for the vast majority of searches conducted on the Internet. Your approach to getting your site listed should include posting your website location and content information to as many sites as possible. You should also spend some extra effort ensuring that your site is correctly listed and positioned in the major top-ten search engines.

Tools of the Trade

The process of registering your website with a search engine can vary dramatically. Trying to manually register your site with as many of them as possible can be frustrating and could take you weeks to complete. To help you with this process, several companies today provide a fee-based service to register your site. Other companies are marketing software that you install on your computer in order to register your site. With my public relations firm, Sierra Communications (www.sierracomm.com), I commissioned a website development company, Flamingo Software (www.flamingo-software.com), to do it for me. It cost me less than one hundred dollars and was well worth it in terms of saving me time and energy. If you choose to have a business register your site for a fee, be certain you understand their methods. Also check references by talking with other site owners who they have helped.

If you choose to go the other route, most of the software manufacturers that create programs for registering your site provide a downloadable trial version of the product. This offering enables you to try out their method prior to making an investment. You can find a listing of software companies and products specializing in search engine registrations by visiting the AltaVista search engine and entering "search engine registration software" (be sure to include the quotation marks) and clicking the search button. A recent inquiry returned 76 matches.

Competing for Position

Securing a better position on a search engine for a specific keyword is the goal of most businesses online today. With better position comes increased traffic to your website. Similar to traditional brick-and-mortar companies, your key to success is location, location, location. In Internet terms, being in the top ten is comparable to a women's wear retail store being located on Fifth Avenue in New York City. Visitors will open your door and visit your site.

Tips That Can Help You Stay on Top

- *Survey your clientele.* Get their perspective on which search engine they use to find subjects that could include your business or organization. Then focus your efforts on those.

- *Know your competition.* If they are positioned at number one on a search engine, they must be doing something right. Consider patterning your site and content after the most successful ones. You can trim hundreds of hours of development time and costs by doing what works well for others. Pay close attention to the keywords and content of their site.

- *Never use frames.* Search engines will not index a frames-based website. Ask your Web designer if they are using a frames-based approach to delivering your website content. If so, find another Web designer quickly!

- *More is better.* The more content you create about your products, services, or organization, the better. Use keywords every chance you get. Although your content may not flow as smoothly as you'd like, having your keywords mentioned often in nonrepetitive sentences can add up to a winning position.

- *Avoid gimmicks.* Spamming search engines with repetitive words (SHOES shoes SHOES shoes) or using multiple pages that have only slightly different content (also called *bridge pages*) are frowned on by the leading search engines. The penalty for trying to trick a search engine into believing your site for cars is larger and more important than General Motors varies by engine. Some ban your site completely from the database, whereas others ignore the content of your site and list your URL without any keywords. Others will ban you from submitting additional sites to their search engine. If you think you've found a gimmick, read the "how to" files on search engines' websites. The chances are good that someone else has tried it before you.

- *Relevance.* The latest buzzword in search engine vernacular is *relevance.* How is the content on your site relevant to the information you initially gave the search engine when you registered?

- *Help is available.* An abundance of information about how to register your website is available at each of the search engine websites. If you are unable to get an answer to your question by reading the information they have posted online, try sending your question via e-mail directly to them. It may take awhile for you to get a response, but most of them will respond eventually.

  The Internet is also a great place to look for handy tips and techniques for improving the ranking of your website with the search engines. Try searching on any of the engines for the keywords "search engine tips." (Use the quotation marks.) A recent query returned 1,572 links to websites containing information about "search engine tips." Your Internet service provider (ISP) and your Web designer are also good sources for information about search engines.

- *Subscribe to periodicals.* If you are serious about marketing your products online, subscribe to periodicals that keep you informed about trends and technology as they apply to the Internet. Many good newsletters and magazines are being distributed electronically over the Internet as eMagazines. See Chapter 12, Free Stuff and Other Resources for examples.

If being at the top of more than one search engine is a requirement, you should consult with a professional Web design house about the construction of your site and your online marketing campaign. Trying to be all things to all search engines is a difficult task. A professional Web design house or marketing firm will be able to develop a marketing strategy designed to get your products or services the attention you desire.

PUBLICITY USING THE WEB

On June 1, 1980, CNN (the Cable News Network) became the first television network to provide news around the world, around the clock. With the increasing popularity of the Internet and the World Wide Web, today's news organizations have adopted similar models—offering fresh news 24 hours a day, seven days a week. Tomorrow's successful news organizations must do the same to stay competitive.

Although the Internet offers unlimited opportunities to get your messages across to the general public, it also makes your messages short-lived. It is no longer effective to simply distribute a press release over a news wire, such as PR Newswire or Business Wire and wait for the journalists to come to you. In fact, if you don't prebrief many journalists, the news is old by the time it hits the wires. The competition among journalists, traditional news media, and online publications will continue to intensify. The good news is that many news organizations also have online divisions so your company or organization can get twice the coverage.

Virtual press rooms have rapidly become a standard feature at most technology industry conferences and have the potential to play a key role in all industries. Virtual Press Office, Inc. (www.virtualpressoffice.com) is an online news management company that facilitates the communications process between high-tech firms and the media. Information is centralized under one virtual roof—or website—to ensure that journalists have the fastest and easiest access to a company's latest press releases, company backgrounders, white papers, and graphics. Access to all the materials is free to journalists, analysts, and industry consultants, and the fee to participating companies is a great bargain at less than $1,000.

Wire services have also begun to use the Internet to their advantage. They embed photographs, logos, and corporate Web addresses into press releases that are made available to journalists over the Internet. Companies continue to forgo the tools of the past—the phone, fax, and e-mail—to make arrangements to distribute their press releases and photographs; they simply go online. PR Newswire has a service called PR Direct, and Business Wire has Business Wire Connect Online. Once a company sets up an account with the wire service, it is able to go to the website; specify the distribution date, time, and news feed; add an attachment; and wait for a telephone confirmation. Technology has made press release distribution much more efficient and effective.

Many leading companies around the world are leveraging the Internet's power to broadcast investor relations events, such as quarterly earnings announcements, shareholder meetings, and investor and analysts' conferences. These broadcasts can be aired live over the Web or recorded and archived on the company's website. Both PR Newswire and Business Wire offer these hosting options. Most companies tend to avoid risk and only broadcast the scripted portion of the conference calls as opposed to the whole call with questions from the financial community.

Finally, tracking press hits continues to get easier as search engines and online services get more sophisticated. Newspapers have gone through the painstaking task of archiving years and years of past articles and placing them on their websites. Magazines continue to do the same. Many people don't realize how simple it is to visit the websites of daily newspapers and magazines to conduct searches for news coverage. Services such as the Electronic Library (www.electroniclibrary.com) also offer unlimited access to hundreds of full-text magazines and newspapers, along with news wires, broadcast transcripts, and other copyrighted content for a low annual membership fee.

ELECTRONIC MAIL—LET'S COMMUNICATE

Electronic mail, or e-mail, is a powerful marketing tool because the unit cost to reach people is low. E-mail is simply a document composed, mailed, received, and read through computers. It first appeared on the computer scene in the 1960s with a program called MAILBOX, installed at the Massachusetts Institute of Technology (MIT). Most e-mail reaches its destination by traveling on the Internet, although office networks, local area networks (LANs), Internet service providers (ISPs), and commercial online services, such as AOL, also provide e-mail services to their users. Most Web browsers have some type of e-mail program. All e-mail programs and services are basically the same regarding features and functionality.

E-mail has rapidly become a tool that is used not only extensively for marketing and publicity purposes, but also by everyone from children wanting to communicate with their grandparents, to senior citizens who use it to go beyond the confines of their homes or care facilities. My parents, now in their late sixties, recently discovered e-mail and are more in touch with old friends than ever before. My in-laws are in their seventies, and they use e-mail as their primary way to communicate with their children and grandchildren who live in different parts of the state and country. E-mail's biggest advantage over postal mail, called *snail mail* by many, is speed. E-mail can be delivered over thousands of miles within seconds or minutes.

One of the biggest marketing advantages of e-mail is that it's scalable, meaning you can reach a lot of people at one time, no matter where they are located in the world. That's a good thing and a bad thing. One of the new words in our vocabulary today is *spam*. It means to indiscriminately send unsolicited e-mail to large groups of people in order to promote a product or service. Unfortunately, spam has often been associated with the practice of scalable e-mail marketing. To many, spamming has become the electronic equivalent of junk mail sent to "Occupant," and it's annoying. I receive at least one dozen junk e-mail messages each day ranging in titles from "New Item: Work at Home!" to "Your ads to millions—We do the work," "Want to get lucky?" and finally from "Wayne" the spam subject line reads "Confirmed." Wayne wanted to host my website for me, and in return, he'd give me free e-commerce services. Great. Fortunately for all of us unsuspecting victims of spam, groups are lobbying for legislation against the practice that may eventually eliminate the problem.

PERMISSION-BASED MARKETING AND OPT-IN ADVERTISING

Spam is an example of how e-mail can be used for marketing efforts in an annoying and negative way. Let's talk about a more positive practice that relies on a trend that, I believe, will soon become the norm for both marketing and public relations. In early 1999, Seth Godin published a book called *Permission Marketing: Turning Strangers into Friends, and Friends into Customers.* The permission-based marketing practice he writes about has also been called "opt-in" marketing and advertising. Simply put, most marketing in the twentieth century was done on an interruption basis—meaning that advertisers interrupted you in order to get your attention. With opt-in marketing, consumers give advertisers their permission to contact them and to share information with them about their latest products and services.

This type of marketing has great value. You can target specific groups of people that meet your demographic needs. These people are not only prequalified, but they are also highly qualified leads who have given you their permission to contact them. They *want* to hear from you, and they are open to what you have to say. So far, e-mail has been the primary technology used for opt-in marketing activities. Some of the more familiar marketing vehicles include electronic newsletters that use e-mail to grab your attention, e-mail messages that embed a live URL to help take you to a website, and online surveys.

E-MAIL NEWSLETTERS

You can get people (preferably interested consumers) to "opt in" to your company or organization's e-mail newsletter through several methods. One of the easiest ways is to take full advantage of your website. As I mentioned before, acquiring website visitors' e-mail addresses and permission to contact them is one of the most important goals of your website. You are already ahead of the game if the consumer has gone to your site looking for more information about your products and services. You can take advantage of this interest to promote your newsletter, which in turn promotes whatever you are selling. Your first task is to make it easy for the visitor to sign up to receive the newsletter. You can create an easy-to-use registration form that asks detailed questions about the visitor's interests and demographics. That information will be useful later when you conduct targeted marketing campaigns. The visitors simply fill out the form, hit the submit button, and then receive the newsletter via e-mail.

One of the best examples of this type of marriage between websites, opt-in marketing, and e-mail newsletters belongs to space.com (www.space.com). I had read that famed CNN/fn financial news anchor Lou Dobbs was leaving his network to start a new educational website on manned and unmanned spaceflight. It was touted as "the only site on the Web devoted to news, information, education, and entertainment focusing entirely on space and space-related content." Space.com was scheduled to be launched on July 20th, the 30th anniversary of Neil Armstrong's historic walk on the moon.

The website offered little information or content except for a two-line form that let people sign up for its daily electronic newsletter, which was to be delivered via e-mail. I signed up online and immediately started receiving an informative electronic briefing on each day's space industry activities. At the end of every newsletter, I was given information on how I could "unsubscribe" if I chose. I was also reminded of space.com's big online debut on July 20, 1999.

The e-mail newsletter, as a precursor to the launch of the actual website, was a great marketing/ promotional tool because it not only piqued my interest, but it also kept me interested for weeks on end. Because I "opted in" to receive space.com's e-mail newsletter, the organization also had permission to contact me about other things via e-mail, such as special events on its website and promotional goodies. On the day of the website launch and then every day thereafter, I continued to receive an e-mail newsletter. This time the newsletter was filled with highlights of what could be found on the site, a live URL that would effortlessly take me to the site, and information about a special section for children that space.com would be starting soon. Space.com continued to draw me in by asking for my help with ideas for the new children's section. I was hooked.

Another example of a creative and effective opt-in e-mail newsletter campaign belonged to one of my previous employers, Metricom, which offered consumers a wireless modem that came equipped with Internet access. During the time I was a part of its marketing department, our president, Don Wood, decided he no longer wanted to send our 20,000 subscribers a monthly paper newsletter. It was too difficult and too expensive to produce. He felt that by the time it was printed and received by the subscribers, the information was relatively old. He suggested an online newsletter that used e-mail as the vehicle for grabbing our subscribers' attention.

Our marketing team created what we thought was a graphically pleasing online newsletter that was easy to read and full of good information. (I'll go into more detail about online newsletters in Chapter 7.) In order to get our subscribers to actually go to the website, we depended heavily on short e-mail messages that we blasted out to them. Now, it may sound as if we spammed our subscribers, but we didn't. All of the subscribers who received the e-mail message had opted in. They had either previously requested more information on our products and services or requested to be put on a list to receive all new information that was made available. Some of them just wanted to belong to a community of other wireless modem users.

One of our challenges was to make the e-mail message attention grabbing. We often struggled to come up with a catchy sentence in the subject line, but somehow we managed, month after month. In the text of the message, we were clear about what the reader would gain from the newsletter. Every sentence in the e-mail message offered some sort of benefit to the reader. Of course, we embedded the URL so that the e-mail recipient would not have to waste any energy going to our website. We also included information about how the recipient could be taken off our e-mail list—again, to make it clear that the recipient had a choice and could "opt out."

CASE STUDY: VIVA LAS VEGAS AND E-MAIL MARKETING

One of my favorite examples of a successful e-mail marketing campaign was by a popular group of Las Vegas hotels and casinos. In December 1998, Mirage Resorts began collecting information from people who enjoyed the corporation's six Las Vegas properties. The corporation used MessageMedia's UnityMail software (www.messagemedia.com), which is a database-enabled list server. Mirage created a virtual guest book on its website (www.mirageresorts.com), which helped people to opt in to e-mail updates about shows and special promotions. Mirage Resorts received tremendous response from people who wanted information proactively delivered to them.

What happened next was remarkable. Mirage Resorts sent an e-mail message to nearly 8,000 people who had opted in, inviting them to take advantage of some special room rates that were available only online. More than 3,500 people clicked on a trackable URL, and out of the 3,500 who saw the complete offer, 2,000 people actually booked rooms. Several weeks later, Mirage Resorts tried again by sending a similar e-mail message to approximately 3,000 people. More than 1,200 people followed suit and booked rooms as a result of the e-mail campaign.

UnityMail made this successful marketing campaign easy. It enabled Mirage Resorts to send individualized, focused messages fast, with powerful, attention-getting graphics to explain promotional offerings, plus a built-in instant-response mechanism. For such an extensive marketing campaign, there was no printing, no duplication, no postage, and no waiting, but there were tools for measuring performance and results.

UnityMail lets companies customize the content of their e-mail message for the interests, buying behavior, or demographics of their targets. UnityMail will send the right content to the right people based on a company's custom-built content database. It delivers trackable Web links, or URLs, in the body of the e-mail to help direct people to a designated website. UnityMail then tracks the people who click on these links. Companies or organizations using UnityMail can send follow-up promotional e-mail messages to those potential customers who did or did not click on the link. This special tracking feature helps ensure high marketing effectiveness.

For Mirage Resorts, the click-through rates on the first e-mail messages were impressive. They received a 47 percent click-through rate on the first mailing and a 42 percent rate on the second.

"The significance of this type of e-mail marketing is that you can send the right message to the right people at the right time," said Walter Thames, director of marketing projects for

MessageMedia. "The Mirage found itself with a highly qualified list of gamers and people who love the hotel and casino. This was a case where we used the brand to its advantage, got permission from potential customers, and ended up with the best response I've ever heard of."

Thames says UnityMail enables companies to present their commercial offerings in a compelling and personal way. He believes it's the ultimate one-to-one marketing, based on consumer buying behaviors. Combine that with the economics, scalability, and instantaneous communications ability of the Internet, and you have a powerful, effective marketing tool.

(Courtesy: MessageMedia)

CASE STUDY: PERMISSION FADES

Written by Nick Usborne, Chief Forking Officer of Forkinthehead Consulting, Inc. (www.forkinthehead.com) and a columnist for ClickZ (www.clickz.com), the leading business-to-business daily online newsletter covering Internet marketing and advertising.

Permission marketing is all the rage right now. In fact, it's so cool that almost everyone is practicing it. Trouble is, a lot of people appear to have forgotten how permission works. Or at least, how it works at its best. Here is an attitude that appears to be prevailing right now. "Hey, we got Nick's permission once, so now we can e-mail him as much as we like." I don't think so. In real life, permission granted isn't a contract; it's a state of mind. The customer's state of mind.

Let me put that concept another way. The moment your customer no longer feels as if you have permission, you no longer have permission, whether you like it or not. The trouble is, in most cases, you'll never get to know when your customer is approaching or has crossed that line. As a result, permission granted can turn into, "How can I get off this dumb list?" before you know it. Long before that moment, the likelihood of your customer responding to any offers falls to almost zero. That gradual erosion of permission sends your conversion rates down the tube in a hurry. For example, I signed up for one of the major points/reward programs awhile back. I was curious to see how it worked.

Here's my experience, as a real-life customer:

1. I went to their site, looked around, and signed up. About two months later, I have no recollection of their site. I don't remember what it looked like. More significantly, I don't remember what I did there. Did I just sign up? Or did I opt in

to receive information on particular areas of interest to me? I have no idea. Just can't remember. This is pretty important, because if I can't remember what permission I granted, then they essentially no longer have my permission. They may think they have it, but in terms of my actual participation in the program, they don't.

2. I waited with anticipation for my first offers. Sure, when permission granted is fresh, it's exciting. In fact, as I recall, I was kind of annoyed that it took them a couple days to get back to me with their first offer.

3. I continued to be interested for about one month. This company sends me an e-mail exactly once every two weeks. To begin with, that felt fine—not too many, not too few. But now? Now I just want to get off the list. Why? Because they let my permission erode, lapse, and collapse.

4. Now I just want them to go away. Trouble is, they don't want me to go. Can I get off the list with one click on the e-mails they send me? Nope. Do they tell me at the end of their mailings how I can say goodbye? Nope. They got me. They want to keep me. And they are going to make it hard for me to leave. Is this smart? Nope. Because now they are spamming me.

Permission withdrawn means that your future e-mails are spam. You can argue that technically I'm wrong. But who cares what you think? It only matters what the customer thinks. If the customer feels as if they're being e-mailed stuff they no longer want, then you're spamming them. So what's the answer?

Think about it this way: If you go on a date and get permission to come your date's home the next evening, have you received permission to go to that person's home every evening for the next five years? No, you haven't. If you want permission granted to translate into long-term sales and a growing return on investment, then you need to keep that permission fresh and renewed. Those points/reward people should give me the opportunity to renew, refresh, or even withdraw my permission on an ongoing basis.

In a permission-based online relationship, the customer's perception is your reality, whether you like it or not. So treat that permission with care—look after it, respect it, renew it, and continue to earn it. Otherwise, the whole concept of permission marketing could quickly descend into another sneaky way to spam people.

(Courtesy: ClickZ)

E-COMMERCIALS

E-commercials have yet to hit the marketing scene in a big way, but they appear to have great potential. E-commercials are highly compressed interactive miniature Web pages that feature audio, video, graphics, HTML links, embedded documents, and computer telephony capabilities. The E-commercial arrives as an executable file that requires no special software to view the message. Recipients simply double-click the e-mail attachment to view the video and engage in each Weblike interface. eCommercial.com, an on-line business, enables advertisers and marketers to reach a qualified set of customers and track precise levels of interactivity in a revolutionary way.

E-commercials also fall into the opt-in marketing category. They only get sent to people who have expressed an interest in a company's product or service. One of the more interesting features of e-commercials are their tracking capabilities. When a campaign is under way, a company can log onto eCommercial.com's secure eComTracker site and view the ongoing results in real time. Because each e-commercial has its own unique identification number, eComTracker monitors activity by the individual user. eComTracker tracks all campaign-related events, including the number of times the message is viewed, message hyperlink activity, message streaming media requests, and transaction activity. It can even follow the path of a single e-commercial as it's passed from user to user. Experts believe that if the content is compelling enough, e-commercials could be an effective marketing tool.

In 1999, Hanson, the Island/Def Jam (Universal Music Group) recording artists, signed an agreement with eCommercial.com to deliver e-commercials to its fans to assist in promoting one of the group's new compact discs. Hanson has an international fan base of millions and has sold 15 million albums and 1.1 million videos worldwide. Demographic reports indicate that the band's teenage fan base are also heavy Internet users, so it will be interesting to track the success of their response to e-commercials.

SIGNATURE ADVERTISING

Signature advertising is something that most of us do without thinking but don't recognize as a viable marketing tool. A signature is a few lines of information at the end of your e-mail message that list your business name, contact information, and even a link to your website. This information automatically appears in every e-mail message you send out, so the visibility potential is great, especially if you participate in online discussion groups.

Many of my colleagues, especially those in sales, use the signature to promote new case studies on their website or to announce the debut of new products and services. The signatures need to be short—about four lines—or else they'll be ignored. They should also be strategic. Above all, be sure to include the link to your site. If you don't, your efforts are worthless. To find out how to create a signature for your e-mail, consult the manual for your browser or e-mail software.

PUBLICITY THROUGH MEDIA RELATIONS

Securing coverage by today's news media has never been easier. Thousands of news vehicles are available, with new print publications and editorial websites springing up daily. Most print and broadcast operations are building or already have complementary online versions that are often expanded. Producers and editors have a 24-hour, seven-day-a-week commitment to fill, and they need to be competitive. They need fresh story angles, breaking news, features, and commentary. They need to fill time and space.

But securing coverage by the news media has also never been harder. Journalists are bombarded daily by hundreds of companies and organizations that have a story to tell—via e-mail. Public relations agencies and independent contractors are out there in the trenches, pitching their clients' stories and vying for coverage in the news. A columnist for *Upside* magazine once told me that he had received 120 e-mail pitches, 13 phone calls, and two overnight delivery packages in one day, all from people wanting free publicity. Any layperson can find a reporter or editor's e-mail address simply by going to the "contact us" section of the news organization's website. Some online publications simplify the contact process by having a direct e-mail connection to the reporter's byline (or name) on the website. Pitching a reporter is as easy as typing a simple e-mail message and clicking on the send button.

Many public relations practitioners rely solely on e-mail as their first line of attack when pitching journalists. They generally follow up with a phone call that is answered by a voice-mail system. Phone calls are rarely returned. For most people, their efforts are lost not on the information highway, but in an information parking lot—a voice- or e-mailbox. Even worse, their pitches may wind up "sight unseen" and victims of the dreaded "delete" button.

Susan MacTavich-Best is, in my humble opinion, one of the masters of this e-mail pitching game. For her, e-mail is a powerful tool. Susan began her career in a high-tech public relations firm in California's Silicon Valley but quickly chose to forgo the security (and in-house politics) of the agency to become an independent contractor. She is also the founder and content creator of a popular San Francisco entertainment website called posthoc.com (www.posthoc.com). Her motto has been and continues to be, "If you want to get coverage from journalists, you have to become a journalist." She is excellent at thinking like one.

Susan's strongest media relations skills fall into the category of e-mail pitching. She rarely does anything using a telephone, and if you actually catch her live via Alexander Graham Bell's 1876 patented technology, you're one of the lucky few. She doesn't care much about punctuation, spelling, or even using upper and lower cases, but she is effective. She cuts through all of the daily e-mail noise by grabbing the reporter's attention in the subject line.

Marc Hausman, founder of Silver Spring, Maryland–based Strategic Communications Group, summed up the whole pitching process best when he said, "The world works on relationships. The Internet and e-mail are just tools." I believe this is true. The most effective e-mail communications with journalists happen when a relationship is already established. Without a relationship, e-mailing journalists is like cold calling. When you have a relationship in place, however, it's like talking with an old friend.

I wish I could be more optimistic about the phone, but I cannot. I know I am making a generality when I say journalists don't return phone calls, but I believe it's true. I have attended many conferences at which journalists unanimously admit they won't call you back unless they have a compelling reason. E-mail is getting to be the same way. Many journalists say you won't get a response from them unless they have a genuine interest in the story you are pitching. It's extremely frustrating. So remember these two important tips when pitching the media via e-mail: First, realize that unless you capture their attention in the subject line, they are not going to open the message. Second, try to establish a relationship with a journalist prior to sending them anything. Your chances of success will increase dramatically.

Chapter 5

PUSH TECHNOLOGY

There have been many media darlings in the world of technology. These are the latest and greatest high-tech tools that receive incredible play in the news media. It's not uncommon to find a technology that is touted as the "next killer application" or a technology that will "revolutionize" the way we live and do business. You hear people talk about technologies and hardware and software tools that will "one day be seamlessly integrated into our lives." There is a lot of hype in the world of high-tech, especially in the intensely competitive business environment in which we have been living in for the past several decades.

One of the technologies to receive widespread media coverage in 1997 was "Push." As the twentieth century drew to a close, most information had traditionally been "pulled" from networks, such as the Internet, by computer users who wanted information. In the case of the Internet, they requested it through a hyperlink. In 1997 Push opened up a whole new way to obtain information. Instead of having to go to a website or requesting information through a search engine, users could subscribe to an information delivery system such as Pointcast (www.pointcast.com).

Users subscribed to channels that would deliver information that was of interest to them. The concept was good. Probably the best way to understand Push is to use the analogy of news delivery. In the good old days, if you wanted to receive a newspaper, you had to physically go to a newsstand and get it. Later, the paper boy delivered the news to your doorstep. That is a simple way to describe how Push worked. In the not-so-olden days, you had to go to a website to find the information you wanted. With Push, it was delivered to your desktop computer automatically, based on the channels to which you subscribed.

POINTCAST

The Push company that received the most media attention in 1997 was Pointcast. With Pointcast, you could subscribe to content that was of interest to you, such as stock quotes, sports scores, news about movies and entertainment or your favorite sports team, the weather in your area, and of course, traditional news headlines. Pointcast's technology actually collected information from its servers at regular intervals and brought it back to your screen. The information could be displayed either as a screensaver that was constantly changing or as a table of contents that you could click on for full stories. More than two million people adopted the free software in less than one year.

Pointcast (and Push companies in general) did not enjoy the limelight for long, however. Going back to the news delivery analogy, the problem with Pointcast is that it delivered the whole newsstand to your doorstep. The technology, at that time, was a network hog—meaning that the constant information retrieval activity could eat up all of a network's bandwidth and bring more traditional work activities to a grinding halt. In addition, the type of information that was delivered to the desktop was "nice to have" but not a "must have." In the business world, some companies chose to ban Pointcast from the workplace because of the bandwidth issue.

In 1998 Push was pronounced dead by the news media. This was unfortunate because in the end, the media's excitement about Push was actually valid. The technology was impressive, but the use of the technology was misdirected and immature. All of the Push companies went silent. Pointcast, which had plans to go public, completely shelved the idea. Two other companies, BackWeb (www.backweb.com) and Marimba (www.marimba.com), spent the year refining the technology and revamping their business propositions.

PUSH RISES FROM THE ASHES

1999 was the year Push rose from the ashes and established itself as a viable "must-have" business solution. BackWeb emerged with its patented Polite Agent™ technology that completely eliminated the bandwidth issues of the past. It provided large corporations, such as US WEST, Cisco, Rite Aid, Schlumberger Dowell, and Pacific Bell, with the ability to proactively deliver time-sensitive, business-critical information to their extended enterprises of customers, partners, and employees. Marimba tried unsuccessfully to distance itself from the Push category and chose to focus its technology on software distribution. Both companies went public in the summer of 1999.

BackWeb further strengthened its core technology that allows businesses to efficiently gather, target, and deliver sizable digital data of any format—audio, video, software files, html, and others—to users' desktops across their extended enterprises. This ability to deliver any size file, "politely" in the background without impacting bandwidth, is already shaping the future of computer-related advertising.

CASE STUDY: THE COMPANY JERK

Written by Mark Gaydos, Instructor, University of California, Berkeley, Extension. Mark Gaydos has more than 13 years of experience in creating and implementing information technology solutions. He is presently director of product management at BackWeb Technologies. Gaydos also teaches software product management for the University of California, Berkeley, Extension. He holds an MBA in Management Science.

When we think of the word jerk, we often think of a rude or obnoxious person. The "jerk" that many companies are thinking about today, however, whether or not they know it, is not a person but instead a key quality of their corporation that makes some companies successful and others inept. In this ever-changing business world, this jerk largely determines a company's ability to adapt and be successful.

If you remember your basic physics, you may recollect that the speed at which an object increases or decreases is known as its acceleration (the change in velocity). So a car that is going 10 miles per hour one moment and then is going 15 miles per hour one hour later is accelerating at 5 miles per hour. However, you probably weren't taught that the rate at which the acceleration changes is called the *jerk*.

Although we use the term jerk loosely, many executives know the value of a positive jerk. In manufacturing, the company's jerk often determines a company's "time to market" or its ability to adapt to business conditions and bring new products to market. One could say that the Japanese auto manufacturers exhibited a positive jerk in the late 1970s when compared to U.S. auto manufacturers who were unable to adapt to changing market conditions as quickly as the Japanese. The U.S. auto manufacturers were therefore left at a serious disadvantage. The well known results of this inability to adapt quickly was that U.S. auto manufacturers lost significant market share and were forced to initiate new programs and methods designed to increase the speed at which they responded to market changes. Today, they are constantly looking at new technologies and methods to increase the speed at which they can adapt to changing markets. In other words, they're looking at new ways to increase the company's jerk.

> The Internet and other new technology, such as Web browsers, have proliferated, thus making information readily available to virtually everyone with whom a company does business, most importantly its customers. Established companies can no longer rest on old business models and antiquated methods of supporting customers or they'll risk losing them to aggressive competitors that leverage the Internet's power.
>
> The best-case scenario in this new economy is that a company will sell to a much more informed and savvy set of customers. The worst-case scenario is that a company loses those customers to a competitor without even knowing what hit them. Such is the case with "brick-and-mortar" publishers that are still reeling from the blow given them by an upstart called Amazon. These companies were actually poised to become the new giant in the electronic marketplace for books, but every single one of them was slow to adapt to change. They had a small jerk or virtually no jerk at all. They also had no ability to respond and adapt quickly to market changes. These companies may not recover.
>
> In the information age, the most important commodity is information, which is the precursor of changing and adapting. Too many companies work obsessively at modifying processes and/or reorganizing in an attempt to be more efficient but have forgotten a basic rule: change cannot occur in a vacuum. In order for any level of an organization to change, information must be acquired and distributed. If an organization is to adapt to change rapidly, it must be provided consistently with critical information.
>
> Today's Push technology has the power to help companies proactively deliver critical information to its customers, partners, and employees. By using technology to increase their jerk, companies can achieve a competitive edge and ultimately rise to their pinnacle of success.

◆ PUSH TECHNOLOGY AND ADVERTISING

In July 1999, BackWeb announced an agreement with Ericsson to embed its technology into Ericsson's Internet Advertiser product. Internet Advertiser was designed to take advantage of BackWeb's patented Polite Agent™ technology as well as its sophisticated attention-management tools. Ericsson's Internet Advertiser is actually a revenue-generating tool for Internet service providers (ISPs) who want to provide Internet access to their subscribers. Internet Advertiser intelligently incorporates a user's submitted profile, geography, and interests and distributes customized advertisements based on the information. Y-Pay, an ISP and advertising service, was the first company to choose this innovative opt-in advertising method.

Based on the business model for commercial radio and television, Y-Pay will provide free Internet access and e-mail to subscribers in exchange for viewing advertisements. Y-Pay will use Ericsson's Internet Advertiser to distribute targeted ads to users' desktops based on individual interests and demographic profiles. Internet Advertiser uses BackWeb's Polite Agent™ Push technology to display ads on subscribers' screens, independent of the website being visited or the application the subscriber is using.

This enhanced Push technology actually eliminates the need for faster personal modems and connections to the Internet because it sends these huge files when the network and/or desktop is idle. When you're working, BackWeb rests. When your computer is idle (or resting), BackWeb works "politely" in the background.

"We believe Ericsson's Internet Advertiser, with BackWeb embedded, will help companies like Y-Pay proactively deliver multimedia-rich files of any size to customers, and will revolutionize the online advertising industry," said Michael L. Sheriff, founder and president of Y-Pay. "Companies can no longer rely on banner advertisements to reach savvy online consumers, they need to deliver information that is pertinent as well as entertaining."

Imagine that you are sitting at your computer screen, using your free Internet service, and waiting for a Web page to download. You are a single male, age 35 with an annual income of more than $75,000. A Lexus automobile drives across your screen (while you are waiting for the page to download). The window rolls down. An attractive woman speaks to you about the merits of the Lexus and gives you a "call to action." This advertisement is entertaining because of the complexity of the graphics and animation; it is informative because you have just learned something new about the performance potential of the automobile; and it's relevant because you are young, single, and rich and would probably love to have a status symbol like the Lexus. You are not annoyed by this "computer commercial" because you agreed to receive it as part of the agreement with the free ISP company.

Ericsson's Internet Advertiser is unique among the industry's advertising and messaging solutions for ISPs because it assures advertisers that they are reaching their target audience. Based on the ISP's customer database of submitted user profiles, Internet Advertiser can distribute targeted movies, rich media messages or "pop up" advertisements, and written or audio messages developed by an ISP or advertiser. Ericsson believes that ISPs need to find unique ways to win in this dynamic marketplace. Internet Advertiser was developed to help service providers generate ad revenues and conduct joint marketing efforts and real-time communication with their customers.

With Internet Advertiser, ISPs can also greatly improve customer service and loyalty. Users can view ads while accessing e-mail, participating in a chat room, or using any other Internet application. Additionally, users can interact with a keystroke or the touch of a mouse to purchase products or services, request more information, or provide feedback to questions. Partnerships between ISPs and companies, such as airlines or banks, can result in a wide range of value-added services for users, including updates on frequent flyer miles or time-sensitive interest rates.

KEEPING CUSTOMERS HAPPY

This type of revitalized Push technology is also going to change the way companies interact with their customers. In the case of Compaq and Hewlett-Packard, they're using Push technology to send software updates and patches to the people who have purchased their computers. Compaq was the first to embrace the technology. It installed BackWeb on all of its Presario computers. The company realized it could save an enormous amount of money by identifying repeatable tech support problems and proactively sending the remedies. The customers never even knew they had a potential problem, and as a result of having the "fix" politely delivered to their machines in the background, they were much happier with their purchase. In addition, the number of repeatable tech support calls went down and customer satisfaction and loyalty went up. Hewlett-Packard quickly followed suit by installing BackWeb on all of its Pavilion line of home PCs.

Another highly effective Push technology feature is BackWeb's attention management capabilities. Attention management is an intelligent notification system that effectively alerts users to the delivery of business-critical information through various display techniques, including tickers and flash notifications. Flashes can be programmed to include multiple levels of interaction from merely notifying a user, to requiring the user to acknowledge the flash, to requiring the user to immediately launch and interact with a designated application before continuing. BackWeb's attention management displays can also be programmed to autoplay according to specific scheduling and expiration parameters, after which the information and associated data can be automatically purged. The attention-capturing technologies create a unique mechanism by which critical information finds users rather than requiring users to find the information. Both Compaq and HP use flashes to alert their customers to new updates and fixes.

CLOSED-LOOP DELIVERY

Closed-loop delivery technology uses BackWeb's Polite Upstream to allow marketers to track, manage, and survey the effectiveness of their messages. For example, marketers can deliver a promotion and an order form to customers and have them electronically returned for fulfillment in a matter of minutes. When the BackWeb server sends a flash or file to users, Polite Upstream enables users to send comments, corrections, or other input back to the server.

The beauty of this technology is that response time is slashed dramatically because customers don't have to click on a URL, wait for the Web page to download, fill out a form, and send it back. The survey is downloaded politely in the background while the customer is doing something else. They fill it out when it pops up and it's instantly sent back to the company. Companies can also track the progress of any delivery or generate reports on the overall usage of the system on a per-user or per-content item basis.

In August 1999, BackWeb introduced a product called BackWeb Rapid Survey as part of its Accelerator suite of Push technology applications. This module improves businesses' responsiveness to employee, partner, and customer feedback by enabling them to publish surveys to collect and analyze information quickly and easily. Surveys are published through a Web-based wizard interface and can be created with questions that have one response, multiple responses, or text answers. The Rapid Survey module takes advantage of BackWeb's flash notifications so companies can capture the user's attention for higher response rates.

Utilizing BackWeb' Polite Upstream, the Rapid Survey module enables two-way publishing or user interaction. With surveys, a publisher sends out a survey "message," then users send back responses from which the BackWeb Rapid Survey module generates a report. In the report, survey results are aggregated, so no manual tallying of data is necessary. Users who have access to view the survey results can see the aggregate data, the raw data by each user, and who actually received the survey and who responded.

PUSH AND PORTALS

In late 1999, US WEST and SAP announced plans to use Push technology to help them "enhance their customers' portal experience." Both companies had made the commitment to build portal sites—SAP would build a site for its business customers and US WEST would build one for its consumers. Despite the different audiences, the technology would be used in similar ways.

The reality of a portal is that no matter how efficient the site is, visitors still must download information. If they are interested in a large file, such as an informational video clip, chances are they will have to wait several minutes for it to download. With Push Technology, its Polite technology leaps into action and delivers the video in the background while the visitor participates in or researches other portal activities and offerings. BackWeb can also be the proactive element of the portal experience because it sends information to portal subscribers before they know they need or want it.

With portals, it's going to be extremely important to offer some sort of differentiation from other portal offerings to achieve a competitive edge. The challenge will be garnering enough attention to get people to choose your portal and then figuring out a way to keep them there. Similar to most Internet-related technology, the ability to capture "eyeballs" will drive advertising revenue and ultimately help make Internet companies successful. US WEST and SAP believe they will be able to make the portal experience easy and accommodating by using this "evolutionized" Push technology.

THE FUTURE OF PUSH TECHNOLOGY

After reading this chapter, you may be asking yourself if most of this priority delivery of information could be done with e-mail. After all, e-mail is ubiquitous and can reach a large audience of thousands of people instantly. The ability to send time-sensitive, business-critical information via e-mail seems like it would be just as effective, if not easier and cheaper.

Picture this scenario: You are sitting at your computer, working intently on a document or surfing the Web. A critical piece of information is sent to you by your CEO, via e-mail, that tells you that he has just sold your company to your arch enemy and stiffest competitor. Unfortunately, you have turned off that annoying "ding" sound that tells you "you've got mail," and you blinked when the e-mail alert popped up on your screen. So there you sit, not knowing that an e-mail message that could change your life forever has just arrived in your mailbox.

Now imagine what the same scenario would be like with Push technology: You are sitting at your computer, working intently on a document or surfing the Web. All of a sudden, a large box full of fiery red flames appears on your screen and won't go away until you click on it. You click, and a video of your CEO appears telling you of the sale of your company to its competitor and letting you know what will happen next. You are informed and better prepared to react to the news.

This technology has unlimited possibilities when it comes to marketing, especially to consumers. For example, Compaq is currently using priority Push technology to send software updates and fixes for repeatable technical support problems. The company has sent more than 13 million communications and fixes. Imagine, though, if Compaq were to use the same technology to send a flash to its customers saying that they are running out of memory. Click here to order this upgrade package and we'll have it delivered to your doorstep in 24 hours.

Throughout this book, you'll find that I talk a lot about the customer one-to-one experience. The Push technology of today and tomorrow will enable companies to better meet the needs of their customers so that they become loyal, lifelong buyers. As we've seen with BackWeb's customers, the ability to communicate and proactively deliver information that is relevant to consumers will impact a company's bottom line and help them improve their image in the consumers' eyes.

Chapter 6

WIRELESS TECHNOLOGY—THE "ANYTIME, ANYWHERE" FACTOR

As increasingly more people join the ranks of the computer literate, they are discovering that they don't always need or want to be tethered to the desktop computer in their home or office. Having the ability to surf the Internet, check e-mail, access files, and participate in live chats or online seminars from locations other than the work station will become a normal way of life. Because of an increase in mobile workers and the remote use of the Internet, GartnerGroup's Dataquest forecasts that the U.S. wireless data market will grow to about 36 million people by the year 2003. In the late 1990s, the Yankee Group (www.yankeegroup.com) reported that one-third of the workforce was already mobile, spending 20 percent or more of their time away from the primary workplace.

Research shows that this flexibility actually increases productivity because it eliminates what is traditionally known as downtime. Imagine being able to get work done while sitting in a doctor's office waiting room or commuting on the train into the city. People want a better mix between their personal and professional lives, and wireless computing helps them achieve that goal.

CHANGING THE WAY WE LIVE, AGAIN

Wireless technology has actually been in existence since the 1970s. Like many technologies, it received its fair amount of hype. According to industry experts, the integration of wireless networks with the Internet and the debut of smart mobile devices will change the way millions of people around the world conduct their businesses and utilize their leisure time. When e-mail and the Internet hit it big in 1995, a small company in Los Gatos, California, was in the right place at the right time to offer consumers a wireless modem and Internet service called Ricochet. From the beginning, Ricochet was the leading technology because it gave computer users complete freedom from wires throughout its coverage areas; it was truly mobile wireless that had the feel of a wired-line connection.

Companies such as ARDIS and Ram Mobile Data Services also offered wireless computing capabilities, but they were either too slow (about 9600 baud), good only for short messages such as stock quotes and sports scores, or too expensive. In many cases, a consumer either paid by the minute or by the amount of data that was sent. Other companies, such as Lockheed, Teledisic, and Hughes Network Systems, are building satellite wireless networks and have promised great wireless data capability, but it hasn't happened yet. When it does, it will only provide you with wireless capability if you are in a fixed location.

In May 1999, 3Com announced that it was shipping the Palm VII organizer, which uses a wireless connection and the new Palm.Net™ wireless service. With this hand-held all-in-one computing device, 3Com announced that users could easily obtain information from the Internet, conduct e-commerce transactions, and send and receive instant messages.

In order to access Internet data on the Palm VII organizer, 3Com reports that a user simply raises the antenna, which calls up a list of applications offered by content providers. By tapping an application icon, the user calls up a new screen known as a "query application." The query application allows the user to define the specific type of information desired—such as a stock quote, flight schedule, or restaurant listing—by selecting from preinstalled options. The user can then send the query to the Internet with a tap of the stylus, and within seconds, a Web "clipping" is returned. A Web clipping is a page of results catered to the user's request and specifically formatted for viewing on the Palm VII screen.

No Wires, Mobile and Fast

In June 1999, Metricom announced a $600 million part-nership deal with MCI WorldCom and Vulcan Ventures (the investing group of Paul Allen, who is the co-founder of Microsoft). Plans called for Metricom and its partners to expand the Ricochet wireless network from three cities (San Francisco, Seattle, and Washington, D.C.) to 46 markets covering more than 100 million people by mid-2001.

Not only would Ricochet eventually be in all major cities, but it would also be lightning fast. The original Ricochet wireless modems offered connection speeds that were comparable to most people's telephone lines—14.4 to 28.8 kilobits per second. The new Ricochet modem and network would continue be wireless (and mobile) at speeds comparable to ISDN lines—about 128 kilobits per second. Soon, Americans would have the luxury of surfing the Net at high speeds, from a park bench. No longer would slow speeds hamper mul-timedia or rich graphics on websites; downloading would be fast, as if you were connected to a high-speed line in the office.

THE FUTURE IS WIRELESS

Today, a consumer's ability to access the Internet and e-mail 24 hours a day, 365 days a year is a God-send to marketers and publicists around the world. Plus, wireless devices can now upload and download e-mail, access online databases, receive scores of information services, and transfer files. More than 100 million pagers, cellular phones, and personal communications services (PCS) phones are now linked to the Internet, some of which have the ability to both receive and send messages. With consumers having high-speed mobile computing and Internet access capabilities, marketers and P.R. pros are using this technology to their advantage.

CASE STUDY: WIRELESS SANTA STATIONS

One of the best examples of how a marketing team used wireless technology effectively can also be attributed to Metricom. In the fourth quarter of 1997, Metricom—the provider of the Ricochet wireless modem and Internet service—was faced with a challenge. The company was in a quiet period because it was focused on developing its next-generation, high-speed wireless network. Local media coverage had diminished considerably. All of the print and electronic media in Ricochet's primary coverage area (the San Francisco Bay area) had already reported on Ricochet and were waiting for the next product announcement. The holiday season was rapidly approaching, and the company wanted to end the year on a high note. It wanted to sell/rent a large quantity of modems and service subscriptions, yet there was no budget for advertising. The company needed a plan that would showcase its products and accomplish its goals.

The first step was to create a media event. According to a survey by the International Mass Retail Association (IMRA), approximately 50 percent of consumers said they planned to do most of their shopping by the first two weeks of December. In addition, an informal survey of shopping malls and centers in the San Francisco Bay area showed that, traditionally, one of the busiest shopping days of the year is the day after Thanksgiving.

The second step was to identify an opportunity. News articles (found online) substantiated the fact that 100 percent of all local bay area newspapers consistently covered retail activity the day after Thanksgiving, with both articles and photographs. Calls to local television and radio newsrooms further verified that news crews would be dispatched to a shopping location on that day (in 1997) and would be looking for a new angle for the annual shopping stories.

The third step was to find a way to seize that opportunity by creating a first-ever holiday event that would almost guarantee public exposure and media coverage. Informal research showed that most malls around the country had yet to offer kids anything more than a chance to sit on Santa's lap and buy a photograph. Metricom was the only company in the nation with the capability to offer full wireless Internet access and e-mail, so the company knew it had a unique opportunity to showcase its product at Christmas. The strategy was to promote the Ricochet wireless modem and Internet service as a communications tool that could be used without wires, anytime and anywhere. Metricom also wanted to use wireless technology to introduce a free, fun, high-tech holiday tradition that would give children a new way to talk to Santa.

Metricom obtained permission to set up two "wireless Santa stations" in front of the Santa House at a popular shopping mall on the day after Thanksgiving, November 28, 1997. The stations consisted of a podium, a laptop, and a wireless modem and enabled children (with the help of their parents) to e-mail Santa three Christmas wishes, free of charge. Metricom volunteers were given media training and instructions for dealing with the public. Metricom's Web team provided Santa with a Ricochet e-mail address and built a "Santa" site to support the activity. The local news media was contacted, as well as on-air radio personalities. Last, a feature-style press release was distributed on PR Newswire.

For 12 hours on the day after Thanksgiving, three shifts of Metricom volunteers assisted children with their holiday e-mail wishes. They answered parents' questions about Metricom's modems and services. They also delivered key messages about Ricochet's ability to communicate wherever and whenever, without wires, and passed out a special holiday promotion flyer.

The results were great. The wireless Santa stations received news coverage from four San Francisco Bay area network-affiliate television news stations, continuous coverage on the number-one news radio station, chatter from local disk jockeys, and an above-the-fold, three-quarter page newspaper article with photograph and graphic re-creation of Metricom's Santa website. The potential reach of the media event was nearly 500,000 San Francisco Bay area residents and equaled approximately $40,000 in advertising dollars. Most significantly, 896 modems were purchased, 450 modems were rented, and 1,346 subscriptions were sold from Thanksgiving until the end of December. The total revenue generated was $420,404. Again, no advertising activity or dollars were spent during that period in the San Francisco Bay area, and it couldn't have been done without wireless technology.

One final note. Upon completion of the wireless media event, Metricom found that it had unwittingly built a database full of children's wishes. From that database, it was able to analyze the information and come up with a top-ten list. The public relations team then crafted and distributed a follow-up press release, "Wireless E-mail Reveals Top-Ten Wishes for Christmas," which was picked up by several news services and publications around the country.

No Restraints

From a marketing point of view, an incredible freedom is associated with wireless technology. How many times have you arranged to participate in a tradeshow in which you've had to spend several hours and hundreds of dollars arranging for a high-speed telephone line so you can demonstrate your product in real time? With wireless capability, you simply plug in and turn on. Wireless also enables you to be creative—to take your products and services beyond the confines of a convention center or office complex to an art and wine festival, to the lobby of a gala event, or to fundraisers where no telephone lines exist. The possibilities are endless.

Even more basic, when you are planning a presentation or demonstration at a client or potential customer's office, how many times have you had to beg to unplug a fax line so that you can secure a connection? The CEO of my husband's company used to carry a 100-foot-long cord with him for presentations, so he could use his computer and the Internet to conduct the live demonstration. He said he felt like an amateur, and his confidence often went down as a result.

NEWS COVERAGE

Journalists are rapidly adopting and embracing wireless technology as well. As the technology momentum was beginning to build in the late 1990s, reporters quickly became savvy to the competitive advantage wireless could provide. My favorite example of this new competitive advantage happened in June 1997. When the Supreme Court announced its landmark ruling overturning the Communications Decency Act, a reporter for *Wired* magazine uploaded the ruling's full text to the Citizens Internet Empowerment Coalition's website from his laptop less than 10 minutes after the verdict was handed down. He did it using a wireless modem. The ruling was on the Web, instantaneously, and it was amazing. The ruling was historical, and so was the method for disseminating critical information in real time.

Here is another example of the way wireless computing is changing the journalism profession. Several journalists I know used wireless modems to help them cover the Microsoft trial. Why? They wanted to achieve a competitive advantage by being the first to report breaking news online. With the Microsoft case, they were able to do it as they sat in the courtroom using wireless technology.

I recall from my days as an aerospace reporter at the Kennedy Space Center, in Florida, another scenario in which wireless would have helped reporters get an edge over the competition. In the late 1980s and early 1990s, the U.S. Air Force used to bus the space reporters out to Cape Canaveral Air Station to witness the launch of Atlas and Delta rockets. A bank of phones was available for use by the press corps. Prior to the actual lift-off, wire service reporters from the Associated Press, United Press International, and Reuters would often write and then dictate their copy to an editor over the phone. They had several variations of the story ready to go, with options for either a successful or unsuccessful lift-off. The reporters would maintain a phone line connection with their news bureaus, and at the time of launch, would give the go-ahead for whichever story was appropriate. The game was trying to beat the other wire services and get your copy on first.

As I joined the masses of high-tech workers in the Silicon Valley, I quickly realized how wireless technology could have, and will one day soon, completely change that whole scenario.

INFLUENCING THE GENERAL PUBLIC

The ability to reach and influence the general public is the traditional focus of marketing and public relations. It's no secret. Radio, television, newspapers, magazines, the telephone, direct mail, billboards, special events, the Internet, and the World Wide Web are the most well-known ways to communicate your messages. But today, trying to change opinion or influence purchasing decisions is harder than ever.

People's opinions are now being influenced by thousands of factors coming at them from everywhere. Companies can no longer afford to rely on just one form of media. They need to take an integrated approach.

ONLINE COMMUNITIES

For as long as humankind has been on this earth, word-of-mouth marketing has been one of the most effective ways to influence the general public. Studies have shown that consumers trust other consumers more than the media, politicians, and companies themselves. That is why online communities, chat rooms, and message boards are so popular. Researchers predict that chat, especially, will become an integral part of consumers' online shopping experiences.

What Is a Community?

To put it simply, a community is a group of like-minded individuals with common interests and goals who gather to interact. An online community is the same thing, however the restrictions of time, geography, or a physical meeting place do not limit the interaction. Chat rooms allow live communication to take place over the Internet or an online service. Message boards and newsgroups allow you to read and post messages. Bulletin board systems, which act as a central source of information, can be accessed with a modem. Users can read or post messages, just like a message board or chat room, but they can also trade software.

These communities can either be a company's best marketing tool or its worst nightmare. Positive threads, or topics of online conversations, can do wonders to spread word-of-mouth referrals about your company's products and services. Negative threads, however, can result in a drop in your stock price, degradation of your company's reputation, or even the boycotting of your company's products and services. These online communities, chat rooms, message boards, newsgroups, and bulletin board systems can provide valuable insight into what consumers, shareholders, and other key influences are thinking about your company.

The next question is how to "manage" these online communities. The bad news is that you can't manage them nor would you want to. Why try to clip the wings of the people who provide you with uncensored feedback? As far as trying to manage negative feedback or word-of-mouth, you can't do it online but you can find other creative ways to address the bad publicity. Negative comments usually focus on problems or perceived problems with your company, product, or service. Start by fixing the problem or perception.

I do not encourage companies to use these community forums to respond to feedback, good or bad. In fact, if your company is publicly traded, then posting comments, good or bad, could be perceived as insider trading by the Securities Exchange Commission (SEC). I know personally of employees who have been fired because they posted innocuous messages on boards. Urge your employees and their families to resist the temptation.

NEWSLETTERS ON YOUR WEBSITE

Online or Web newsletters, if done properly, can be useful tools for influencing the general public. As we have discussed previously, the most important job you have when producing an online newsletter is to make sure everything you write has a benefit to the reader.

When I was at Metricom, our online newsletter was called *Ricochet Unwired.* Each month, we sent an e-mail message to our subscribers who had asked to be sent new information relating to their wireless modems. We included a URL that quickly carried them to a graphically pleasing Web page. The online newsletter was not very long—probably about the length of two computer screens. We didn't want our audience to feel like they were reading a tome or had to invest a lot of time.

Unwired had one feature article, three customer success stories, technical tips, links to other websites that provided topical information for that month, a short message from a senior-level executive, and a three- or four-question survey. The three customer success stories eventually evolved into a contest in which we offered three months of free service to the provider of the most useful testimonial. It was all information that purposely offered great value to the reader.

We never realized the significance of this Web newsletter until the company stopped doing it. Our newsletter team always thought of it as a monthly annoyance. To the 20,000 subscribers of our company's wireless Internet service, however, it was not only appreciated but also missed when it ended. The content creator, Becky Perkins, received several complaints and questions about its whereabouts. The letters and e-mail messages acknowledged that the product users actually did read the newsletter every month and learned from it.

In my opinion, the demise of *Unwired* was a great company loss as well. Gone was the ability to touch the customer on a regular basis. The subscribers had opted in to receive the newsletter in the first place, and it was an effective communications vehicle. The benefits to the company were numerous. *Unwired* served as a way to advertise new promotions such as the referral program and our special deals on wireless modems. It was an invaluable monthly research tool because we always included a mini-survey as part of the newsletter. That mini-survey provided a wealth of information for the product marketing group as it tried to figure out what features and services they needed to provide in the future.

After I left the company, I heard that it was planning to go back to sending out hard copy paper newsletters. I have always felt that paper newsletters are expensive, time consuming to produce, and often obsolete by the time they reach the audience's mailboxes. I also think value is lost because paper newsletters do not offer any instant feedback capability.

Today's Web and e-mail newsletters seem to be becoming widely accepted by the general public. They're quick and easy to read, they don't require a huge investment of time by either the reader or the producer, and they're inexpensive to produce. I subscribe to at least three or four e-mail newsletters and would love to see more Web newsletters. They're informative, pleasing to the eye, and provide valuable content on a regular basis.

◆ ELECTRONIC AND ONLINE SURVEYS

Marketers are increasingly becoming smarter in the way they obtain information from consumers. How many times have you received a call from a researcher asking if you would mind taking a 30-second phone survey? I always go for it because it's easy and doesn't require a lot of my time. Surveys, in general, can be an effective lead-generation tool for products and services as well as provide sound information for product development and marketing. If they are designed well, they can generate high response rates. They can even have great public relations value and serve as the launch pad for publicity campaigns.

In the past, traditional survey techniques involved the telephone, mail questionnaires, and person-on-the-street interviews. But recently, I have received several e-mail messages asking me to take part in quick online surveys. The most effective one I have received thus far was from a public relations organization that hired Mediamark Research to survey public relations professionals on a few key issues.

This request caught my attention so much that I kept the actual e-mail message I received because I thought it was effective. It said, "You have been randomly selected to participate in this survey that will take no more than eight minutes, and you will also have the chance to win $1,000. Simply click on the URL below (or paste the address into your browser) to begin. Thank you for taking a few minutes to complete the survey, you will be entered to win $1,000. If you prefer not to receive future survey invitations, please reply and write 'remove list' in the body of the message. Thank you in advance."

I thought the e-mail message was brilliant. Who doesn't want to win $1,000? Who doesn't mind spending eight minutes on a survey that is relevant to you? I went to the URL and found a very user-friendly questionnaire that required me to click on multiple choice answers. It was visually pleasing, easy to complete, and actually took less than eight minutes.

ELECTRONIC POSTCARDS

The jury is still out on whether electronic or digital postcards can actually help you to improve your bottom line, but they seem to be effective in building brand awareness. The theory behind electronic postcards is that they're supposed to greatly increase your website's exposure through links to your home page. It's theorized that postcard recipients will visit your site, be exposed to your advertisers (and other products and services), and send one or more cards themselves.

The first time I learned about electronic postcards was in 1997. I had been out of the aerospace business for a year or so and had lost touch with what was going on in that industry. There really wasn't much of a buzz around space exploration beyond the boundaries of places like the Kennedy Space Center and Houston's "Mission Control." The aerospace community realized that lack of larger community interest and awareness and got together to create an annual tribute to the people who, through their space-related work, have contributed so much to science, medicine, and everyday life.

A friend of mine, from Kennedy, sent me an electronic postcard from "beyond the edge of the universe." Actually, it was an e-mail notification telling me that I had been sent a postcard "from space." It instructed me to click on an embedded URL to pick up the card. I did, and it was pretty neat. It looked like a traditional postcard but it was all on the Web.

Beyond the card, I discovered that the rest of the website was dedicated to Space Day (www.spaceday.com). It offered Webcasts on various interesting space-related subjects. There was a big section for teachers, which included an online survey so that Space Day organizers could gather input on educator's needs and desires. There was a "mission update" section for visitors to learn about the latest and greatest space activities. Finally, there was a "Friends of Space Day" section in which people could help promote the cause on an annual basis.

The U.S. Open is another example of an organization that used electronic postcards as a way to publicize its sporting event and to generate more traffic to its website. In 1998, the U.S. Open used its website to invite the general public to interact with the players via electronic postcards. The plan was successful and received a great response. It's reported that tennis star Patrick Rafter received more electronic postcards from fans than any other player in the tournament, with a final tally of 3,000.

INCENTIVES AND PROMOTIONS

As the effectiveness of banner ads is continually questioned and the click-through rates decline, more websites are offering frequent-user programs, online coupons, sweepstakes, and other incentives to attract and keep customers. The goal is to increase customer acquisition rates, improve brand loyalty, and capture more consumer data that can be used for market research.

The types of companies offering online incentives vary. Cool Savings, Cybergold, MyPoints, and Netcentives are a few of the companies that offer consumers points, instant discounts, and actual cash rewards in exchange for information or purchases. Travel sites and Web merchants were among the first to offer incentives, but others are following. Hot new portals as well as traditional retailers and financial institutions are also climbing on board the incentive bandwagon.

Incentives enable marketers and merchants to appeal more directly to consumers and turn visitors into buyers and buyers into loyal customers. Customers receive points for everything from making a purchase to registering software. Another important trend is the use of the online coupon. According to a recent NPD Online Research poll, 31 percent of Internet users said they have downloaded coupons from the Web. Fifty-six percent of savvy online users said they'd be more likely to do business with a website if it offered some type of loyalty program.

Netcentives™ is the leading developer of online rewards and loyalty programs in today's new era of e-commerce. It's ClickRewards™ is the only Web loyalty program to reward consumers with frequent flyer miles on all of the major U.S. airlines. The eight major airlines that have exclusive part-nership agreements with ClickRewards represent 93 percent of the total frequent flyer market.

ClickRewards uses technology to track its program results. Merchants have access to real-time transaction summaries, 24 hours a day, seven days a week. Click Rewards also offers security. It has a patented, application-layer security solution that enables complete message privacy and high standards of message authentication. This turnkey solution includes promotion design and consulting, software implementation, real-time account monitoring and reporting, reward fulfillment, and customer service. Netcentives customers include barnesandnoble.com, Beyond.com, E*TRADE, garden.com, Macy's.com, msn shopping, OfficeMax.com, PlanetRx, Preview Travel, and Yahoo!

CASE STUDY: WEBSTAKES.COM AND THE SHARPER IMAGE LAUNCH INTEGRATED PROMOTIONAL SWEEPSTAKES ON THE WEB

On August 6, 1999, Webstakes.com, a leading online sweepstakes promotions company, ran a new Private Label promotion integrating both offline and online promotional tools for The Sharper Image stores, print catalog, and website (sharperimage.com).

The Sharper Image's "Win the Chair" Sweepstakes, in which six entrants won a new Quad Roller Get-A-Way Massage Chair from The Sharper Image, was an integrated offline and online promotion tying together in-store promotional displays and catalog branding with an interactive online promotion created by Webstakes.com. All three components were used to drive customers to The Sharper Image's website. Customers entered to win through in-store and catalog entry forms or on the Sharper Image website at www.sharperimage.com. Through the "Win the Chair" sweepstakes, The Sharper Image drew customers online with a branding effort to help The Sharper Image build loyalty with its customers across multiple media platforms. In addition, Webstakes.com collected the e-mail addresses of both online and offline entrants and built an extensive opt-in database, which was designed to help The Sharper Image target customers more effectively.

"We partnered with Webstakes.com in an effort to expand our online outreach and invite new and existing consumers to experience The Sharper Image's entertaining and technologically advanced website," states Meredith Medland, director of the

Internet division for the Sharper Image. "Webstakes.com's online promotions and sweepstakes administrative experience offered the most complete coverage of the marketing channels across the board."

(Courtesy: Webstakes.com)

TELEVISION

Television, despite its new competition with computers and the Internet, continues to be big business in the advertising world. In 1998, Nielsen Media Research estimated that the total number of television households in the United States (including Alaska and Hawaii) was almost 100 million. Remember, that's households, not individuals. The amount of money generated by local and national advertising spending reportedly equaled approximately $44 billion each year.

Television holds incredible power, especially because it is a visual medium that can have a profound affect on emotions. I recently read Lesley Stahl's book *Reporting Live* Stahls has been a television journalist with CBS for more than two decades. In her book, she tells the story of how she prepared a five-minute, 40-second report that was highly critical of President Ronald Reagan. After it aired, she said she thought the phone would ring off the hook with negative comments from the President's advisers. Instead, she received congratulatory calls from them, thanking her for a great story. They loved it.

She went on to say that the video of the President was so powerful and emotional that no one paid attention to her words. Later, a focus group saw the story without narration and thought it was either an ad for his political campaign or a positive news story.

Television also has an incredible power to influence. I have seen family and friends fall victim to the power of infomercials. It's easy to get sucked in. There you are, clicking through the channels with your remote control and you stop on an infomercial. The next thing you know, you have watched the whole thing. By the end of the program, you may be thinking that the product sounds pretty darn good. The next time you happen across the informercial, you stop on it again. You listen. Sometimes you actually break down and buy the product. Infomercials make it easy to get caught up in the excitement and enthusiasm of the host.

AN INTEGRATED MARKETING MIX

The combination of e-mail, the World Wide Web, radio, television, and print will clearly continue to be an unstoppable force in our publicity and marketing activities of tomorrow. Companies are becoming increasingly more sophisticated in their use of all of these elements.

Moving the Herd

Just the other night I was watching one of the primetime, network television news programs. It produced a story on an author who had some controversial thoughts on raising children. In the recent past, it had become commonplace at the end of the broadcast to direct the audience to the program's website to learn more about the report. But this time, the program host not only invited the audience to visit the site, but also to participate in a live online chat session with the author on a designated day later in the week.

I thought this move was strategic because it not only pointed the television viewing audience to the website, but it also gave them a reason to return to the site on a given day and to stay. It sent the message that the news program took its commitment to inform and educate its audience seriously. It sent the message that it wanted audience participation.

In the end, the online chat strategy accomplishes several things. It's the extra touch that helps increase television-viewing loyalty, which in turns means higher ratings, which ultimately, means greater advertising revenue. It's a powerful tool used to capture the television-viewing audience and turn them into regular website visitors. Once on the site, there would be promotional information that would point the audience back to the television show. It is an effective circle of communication.

The Power of the URL

Not so long ago, it used be that a catchy and memorable telephone number, such as 1-800-CALL-ATT or 1-800-GO-WIRELESS, used to be one of the most effective ways to get an audience to respond to a marketing call to action. Today, you can't listen to a radio advertisement, view a television ad, or read a print ad without finding some reference to a website. Companies have quickly learned the value of supplementing these advertising forms with an online presence.

Toward the end of the 1990s, the race was on to secure Web addresses that were either logical names that reflected a company's business, such as www.ibm.com or www.etoys.com, or were just plain catchy, such as www.talkingbird.com. When my husband and I were trying to secure a domain name for our public relations and marketing firm, we found that a lot of our top choices had already been taken. And that was just the "dot coms." The "dot nets" (www.xxxx.net) were also being snapped up at an incredible rate.

In order to influence the general public today, you must first get them to your site with that catchy or easy-to-remember Web address, and then you must keep them there. One of the best examples I have seen of getting people to stay on a site is Ask Jeeves. First of all, the company secured not one, but two addresses, www.ask.com and www.askjeeves.com. That way, Web surfers have two chances of actually getting to the site.

Ask Jeeves is an information-retrieval site that draws from an extensive knowledge base of millions of answers to the most commonly asked questions, from people all over the world. Once consumers are on the site, they rarely leave. Everything they need can be found there. Ask Jeeves' technology enables the company to deliver you to another company's website, but that website is always framed by Ask Jeeves. If you want Ask Jeeves to take you to another site or if you want to ask another question, you have the capability right there on your computer screen. In addition, Ask Jeeves continues to run banner ads in its frame, thus it continues to have an advertising revenue stream.

The Quadruple Whammy

As a public relations professional in the high-tech field, I constantly read and thumb through about a dozen trade and business print publications. As I was reading one of these magazines, I noticed an advertisement from Seth Godin, the author of *Permission Marketing*. It showed a picture of his book cover and gave a short summary. It also displayed a graphic that offered four free chapters of the book. All you had to do was to e-mail him. I did it, and within a few minutes I received an e-mail message that included the free chapters and gave me links to Amazon.com and barnesandnoble.com that would enable me to easily purchase the entire book. He included the links in the greetings message and then at the end of the four chapters.

To break this tactic down, Godin first used his own permission marketing theory. He advertised in print and gave me an incentive to provide him with my e-mail and contact information. His e-mail message not only hooked me as a potential buyer of his book, but also directed me to two e-commerce websites where I could easily purchase the book. Finally, as part of the content of the book, he once again encouraged readers to e-mail him at a specific e-mail address so that they could receive updates "on what the future holds for permission marketing online." One, two, three, four. Print advertising, e-mail, Web, book. In addition, I was now in his database of potential future book buyers.

Politics

Technology, especially the Internet, has pervaded through the world of politics in a big way. The Office of the President of the United States has a website. Members of Congress have websites. Even local city council members and school board officials often have websites. This use of technology can be extremely effective for educating voters, raising funds for upcoming campaigns, and disclosing politicians views on important issues.

I recently visited the website of Tom Campbell (www.campbell.org), who is the current Representative of California's fifteenth congressional district—my district. He used his site to introduce himself and to post his track record as a public servant. He had a section on his legislative record, on where he stood on various issues, on upcoming town meetings and events he would be either hosting or attending, and on ways the general public could lend financial support to his campaign. When I last checked, 413 members of the House of Representatives had similar websites.

CASE STUDY: GARTNERGROUP'S DATAQUEST SEES PIVOTAL ROLE FOR INTERNET IN PRESIDENTIAL ELECTION IN 2000, BUT ONLY IF CANDIDATES LEARN FROM PORTALS, E-COMMERCE SITES

In the 1930s, the then-new medium of radio powered Franklin Delano Roosevelt to the presidency. In the 1960s, television, still in its infancy, swung the tide for a victorious John F. Kennedy. The Internet is the new kid on the block, and it is poised to play a major role in presidential politics in the year 2000. According to GartnerGroup's Dataquest, the issue will not be if candidates use the Internet, for virtually every candidate will have a website. The key will be who masters the medium most effectively. The challenge facing candidates is to exploit this new Internet medium to its fullest—to capture the "hearts and minds" of the voters as FDR and JFK did with radio and TV, respectively.

In terms of pure numbers, the Internet's importance is assured. According to a recent Dataquest survey of 16,500 U.S. households, 55 percent of voting-age Americans have Internet access from somewhere, be it home, work, school, or elsewhere. That figure was projected to rise rapidly to 63 percent by "Super Tuesday" (March 7, 2000), when primary elections and caucuses will choose more than half the convention delegates needed to secure the major party nominations. By election day (November 7, 2000), 70 percent of voting-age adults were expected to have Internet access. The survey also found that approximately 12 percent of Web users regularly visit sites about political candidates, a figure that was sure to rise as election day drew nearer.

As an interactive medium with graphics, video, and audio capabilities well beyond those of print, radio, or TV, the Internet seems ready made to deliver candidates' messages in a dramatic and memorable way. However, graphics, audio, and video can require extensive download times, particularly considering the limited download speeds in most U.S. households. As previously mentioned, long download times can discourage visitors from staying on or returning to the site.

Another major advantage of the Internet is its interactivity—its ability to gather information about voters: their likes, dislikes, and attitudes. However, this ability is a double-edged sword as well—as Al Gore recently discovered after the negative publicity caused by press reports that his "Gore2000" website contained questions soliciting information from children without parental permission. This tactic proved to be a serious error since 40 percent of those who visit political websites are from households with children under 18.

The challenge facing candidates in 2000 will be to gain the advantage by going beyond "plain vanilla" websites and fully exploiting the Internet's capacity to capture the voters' hearts and minds. Just as Kennedy drew upon the experience of the "image doctors" of his time, GartnerGroup's Dataquest suggests that candidates draw upon today's Internet experts to:

- Capitalize on the lessons learned in the development of portal services and e-commerce sites by developing site "stickiness" through compelling interactive content.

- Make effective use of graphics, audio, and video while striking an optimum balance between an appealing site and fast download times.

- Tread lightly while garnering voter information by employing alternative personal data-gathering methods such as competitions, free newsletter subscriptions, and surveys on topical issues.

  GartnerGroup's Dataquest went on to report that if no candidate successfully masters the Internet in this election, then the first "Internet presidential election" may have to be postponed to 2004.

(Courtesy: GartnerGroup)

APPROACHING THE NEWS MEDIA

When you think of free publicity, the simplest and most obvious way to obtain it is through the news media. It is not difficult to secure coverage of your products and services, special events, causes, or even your personal views and opinions by convincing a reporter, editor, or producer that your story is newsworthy. And news coverage is free. So how should you do it, and what technologies should you use to improve your chances?

There is a common myth that all news organizations have the latest and greatest technology. We'd like to believe that myth because information delivery can be instantaneous, thanks to the Internet. One would also like to think that all news reporters are equipped with laptop computers, cell phones, and wireless modems so they have access to breaking news and background research, but they don't. As the end of the twentieth century approached, many television news reporters continued to take notes on paper and dictate their scripts over the phone to some poor intern who would retype the copy for broadcast. Television newsrooms also continued to depend heavily on the fax machine to learn of upcoming news events, press conferences, and availability of video news releases. Many news organizations are still trying desperately to get up to speed, but for most, the process is slow because of budget issues.

E-MAIL

In previous chapters, we talked about e-mail. You learned that the quickest way to capture a journalist's interest, using e-mail, was through the subject line, followed by a succinct, well-conceived pitch. Many marketing and public relations professionals send one or two e-mail pitches and then follow up with a phone call. Feedback is rare unless you have an established relationship with the journalist.

E-mail has been broadly accepted by the news media, with the exception of a few holdouts. In mid-1999, I read a story about a prominent *New York Daily News* editor who actually bragged that she had never opened her e-mailbox. This editor claimed to receive three of the large plastic boxes (that the U.S. Post Office uses to deliver large quantities of mail) every day. She was quoted as saying that with traditional mail, faxes, and phone calls, she didn't need a fourth way "for public relations people to get a hold of her." I thought she had an interesting and somewhat old-fashioned attitude.

Most reporters—print, online, and broadcast—however, now have e-mail addresses that are made available to the public. So you don't like a reporter's story? Simply go to the website, find the reporter's e-mail address, and send your comments.

The e-mail addresses can be found on the electronic masthead, under the "contact us" or editorial information section and even at the end of their stories. Some publications are so interested in your comments and feedback that they will provide a link to a reporter's e-mail address.

How to Use E-mail Effectively with the News Media

E-mail is rapidly becoming the most popular way to alert news organizations to upcoming events or to pitch a story idea. Many print and online journalists prefer e-mail as their first point of contact. Having been a journalist, I can see several benefits to being "pitched" this way. First, e-mail can be read quickly. Print and online journalists receive dozens of pitches from public relations practitioners, marketers, industry executives, and the general public each day. If the e-mail pitch is written well, they can easily determine if they want to pursue the idea after reading just a few short sentences. E-mail pitches are easy to wade through and take far less time than listening to voice-mail messages or talking to people on the phone. The bad part for the person pitching the news event or story idea is that journalists usually only respond to e-mail pitches if they are interested. You rarely receive a courtesy rejection e-mail response.

E-mail can be an effective tool for successful relationship building as well. As a marketer and public relations professional, I tend to read several trade magazines and the business/technology section of some of the nation's top-tier daily newspapers. When I read a story that interests me, especially if a reporter with whom I'd like to establish a relationship writes it, I send a quick e-mail commenting on the merits of the story and the reporting style. Too often reporters receive little or no feedback on stories that they have put their hearts and souls into. They truly appreciate feedback because it helps them improve their craft.

Another idea to keep in mind is that a quick e-mail message can often be the vehicle for providing reporters with more valuable information. For example, you may read an article by a reporter who has a specific beat or area of expertise. If the reporter continually follows a trend, the follow-up e-mail may provide story ideas or information that can be incorporated into future articles or broadcasts. Your courtesy e-mail may not produce immediate results, but it can be useful in building helpful, valuable relationships.

On the flip side, e-mail has also become the first line of contact for many journalists when approaching companies and organizations. For them, it's fast and efficient. Just like you, they can easily go to a website and find a contact name and e-mail address. With the click of a mouse they can request information, confirm facts, set up phone or in-person interviews, or even interview you with an e-mail questionnaire. If you're smart about using e-mail as a communications vehicle for working with journalists, you'll understand that a quick response time is essential for meeting deadlines and building relationships.

It's also important to understand that you can create or shape perceptions with e-mail. Credibility is easily lost if your message reads as if a second grader wrote it. A lot has been written about e-mail etiquette, so before you push the "send" button, be sure to reread your message. You'll want to make sure your spelling, grammar, and punctuation are correct. You'll also want to read your message out loud to check the tone, or voice, of the message. Little things, like writing in all capital letters, can send a message of anger or disgust. Writing in lower case can send the message that you are extremely casual. It can also say that you're too lazy or apathetic to take the time to craft a professional message.

Finally, it's crucial to remember that when communicating with journalists via e-mail, everything is "on the record" and fair game. Your written word, sent via e-mail, can be used as a quote or paraphrased and published. You need to be careful what you write, even when sending a casual personal note. Again, everything is on the record, no matter who you are.

Some More Tips

- Never send out a mass e-mail pitch. Most print and online publications are highly competitive and do not appreciate nonexclusive story ideas. If you have an actual news event, then it is fair game to alert all of the publications and news organizations on your target media list.

- When replying to a journalist, always double-check to make sure that you have not copied all of the recipients who may have received the original e-mail message. Sometimes your reply may not be meant for all eyes.

- Before hitting the send button, double-check the message for spelling, punctuation, and grammar. Also, if you get into the practice of reading your e-mail messages out loud, you will catch mistakes and hear the tone of the message.

- If you are sending the same e-mail message to several journalists or news organizations and you use the cut-and-paste capability of your word processor, be sure to double-check the content. It can be a major blunder to send a message meant for one journalist to another. Often, the damage to the relationship is irreversible. Plus, it's embarrassing when you're caught.

- Don't send jokes to journalists. They are already bombarded with far too many e-mail messages on any given day.

- Don't send electronic postcards to journalists. They really get annoyed when they find themselves automatically and unknowingly downloading a large file, especially one that is PR-oriented.

- Create an attention-grabbing subject line. Then, put the most important information in the first two sentences of the first paragraph. Assume that is all the reporter will see.

◆ PRESS KITS

It used to be that a well-developed press kit was enough of an educational tool to get a reporter interested in your company, organization, politician, or celebrity. The press kit contained the latest press releases, marketing collateral, photographs or slides, logo slicks, fact sheets, and biographies. Later, people often included computer disks and a CD-ROM after they became more popular. Press kits contained a wealth information and journalists were happy. In fact, it was considered routine for journalists to ask for press kits before they made any kind of commitment to doing a story or covering an event.

Needless to say, a lot of trees were wasted as reporters collected press kit after press kit. As time went by, the press kits became more elaborate and expensive to produce. I remember going to hear a young, high-tech television reporter, Scott Budman, from KNTV-San Jose, talk to a group of wide-eyed public relations professionals in early 1999. He held up a slick press kit that contained everything he could ever want—background information, customer testimonials, and a CD-ROM packed with presentations, videos and graphics, photographs, and reproducible graphics. Much to the audience's chagrin, he said he never read or looked at a single item in that press kit. What he wanted from publicity seekers was a single piece of paper that succinctly told him about the subject. That was all he had time for, and that was all he wanted. It was a hard lesson to swallow.

The other message he delivered was that all of the information that normally goes into a press kit should be made available online through a website. It is far easier (and quicker) for reporters to research online because they don't have to fuss with papers or disks or a CD-ROM. For them, time is a valuable commodity because of continuously looming deadlines.

We may continue to see traditional press kits at places like tradeshows or conferences, but not for long. I admit some people may still want to take hard copy press kits with them. Journalists may even ask you to mail them a press kit. For some, I know for a fact that this request is just a polite way to get you out of their hair. Having picked up many a press kit myself, I can personally tell you that I rarely read any of them. They became trash can fodder.

Many press kits of today are paperless and can now be found in virtual press offices, hosted either by commercial companies or on your own website. They offer four or five of the latest press releases, company backgrounders, white papers, logos, photographs, and graphics. Streaming audio and video will soon begin popping up as additional elements on virtual press office sites. Highlights of speeches and presentations, along with PowerPoint slide shows, will be archived there so reporters can see and hear what they may have missed in person. Everything a journalist could possibly need or want will be found at these sites.

Companies such as Virtual Press Office, Inc., one of the leading online news management companies in the United States, not only help organizations make the information available to journalists but also set up computer terminals at tradeshows and conferences so online access is free and easy. The bottom line is that tomorrow's journalist won't have to carry any equipment or paper in order to get access to current and historical information at these kinds of events.

OVERNIGHT DELIVERIES AND SNAIL MAIL

It used to be that when you received a letter or package using an overnight delivery service, you knew it was important. Someone had taken the time and expense to make sure you received it the next business day. I think it's safe to say that most people would open the package immediately. Journalists also counted on these overnight services to deliver critical information, video, photographs, and graphics to them so they could meet their deadlines. In the mid-1990s, public relations practitioners and publicity hounds figured out that this form of delivery was a sure-fire way to get journalists' attention.

This technique worked for awhile, until journalists and entire newsrooms started being bombarded with FedEx, DSL, Airborne, and UPS overnight shipments. By 1999, many journalists admitted that they had dozens of these packages stacked up in their offices, unopened. The so-called "critical" information was no longer critical. Journalists depended on e-mail and the Internet to get the data they needed.

While electronic information overload and priority overnight deliveries hit the news business in a big way, a funny thing happened with regular U.S. postal mail. By 1999, many journalists no longer received piles of letters and flyers. Snail mail, as technology-savvy individuals fondly call it, had dwindled considerably. I once attended an industry conference for professional marketers and public relations people and heard two top-tier journalists from *Forbes and Fortune* magazines talk about how they actually missed the traditional mail. This new development provided the edge I needed to get my story ideas, pitches, and news events across. I started supplementing my creative e-mail pitches with attention-grabbing direct mail campaigns via the U.S. Post Office.

One of my favorite campaigns involved a postcard that I had professionally printed while I was at BackWeb. As I mentioned in Chapter 5, BackWeb had been in the consumer Push business in 1997 and was lumped into a group with other Push companies. The technology had been hyped by the media, then pronounced dead a year later. BackWeb had gone silent, like a submarine, in 1998 only to emerge a viable leader in the Push technology market in 1999. Push had evolved into an important technology that would shape the business-to-business, business-to-consumer, and business-to-employee markets.

The postcard I sent to more than 400 journalists and industry analysts was big and black as night. The front read: "The reports of my death have been greatly exaggerated." Push Technology, 1999. It was a play on a famous quote by Mark Twain. The back of the card was blank except for BackWeb's URL. I had room to write a message on the back, so I used it to notify my target audience of an upcoming panel of BackWeb customers at Internet World Summer '99. I knew I had gotten through when a colleague of mine received an e-mail message from a prominent industry analyst who thought it was very creative. The bottom line is that snail mail actually caught her attention.

My point is that sometimes you have to figure out how to come in through the back door. As I found out, supplementing high-tech with some of the more conventional communication methods of the past turned out to be a winner. I also want to recommend that you try to put yourself in situations where you can talk to and learn about the media. You will often pick up little gems like I did that help you rise above the noise.

MORE ABOUT VOICE MAIL

What can I say about voice mail? Almost nothing good when it comes to serving as a communications tool for reaching the media. What I am about to say next comes from personal experience. I was a journalist. Most of my friends are journalists. I work with journalists daily. Here it goes. The majority of working journalists today do not return phone calls. And they are the first to admit it.

I'll never forget a column I read that was written by a smug former senior editor of *PC Week* magazine. It was called "Why Editors Don't Call Back." The former newsman (ironically now a self-proclaimed marketing and PR guru) told the story of how he was invited to address this very subject at a marketing communications gathering in Canada. He said he told the audience lame jokes about the editors going on vacation and forgetting to change their voice mail, or about the editors being too busy rock-climbing, or about being "miffed" at the mispronunciation of their last names by P.R. professionals. He never answered the question.

Some journalists have a legitimate reason for not returning phone calls. They just don't have the time. They have stories to write and deadlines to meet. You can leave a message on voice mail with your pitch and your phone number, but usually the only time they will call you back is when they find your story idea or news event compelling. A big disadvantage to using voice mail to try to garner news coverage is that it does absolutely nothing to help you build a personal relationship.

The key to success when pitching journalists via the phone is to find out what their schedules are and work around them. Try to discover if they have a daily or weekly deadline. If it's a weekly deadline, then do not call on the days when you know they'll be crunching. Also, try to find out what time of the day they're most likely to be enjoying a relatively calm period at their desks.

◆ EDITORIAL CALENDARS

Most print magazines and some daily newspapers create what is called an *editorial calendar*. This is a rundown of the upcoming article topics and special-issue focuses they have scheduled for the year. It used to be that you could only get these editorial calendars by requesting an advertising media kit, but technology has changed that practice. Most editorial calendars are now available online at the publication's website or through media services such as EdCals.com (www.edcals.com).

I have found most editorial calendars to be quite thorough. When I was investigating a business and information technology publication called *CIO,* I was pleased to find not only a detailed calendar but also several pages of notes on how to pitch the magazine. *CIO* also included strategic do's and don'ts. The obvious benefit of providing an editorial calendar and some pitching advice—especially online—is to dramatically reduce the number of inquiries from people wanting to know when and how to approach your news operation.

Bacon's Information and Media Map have developed a specialized subscription-based editorial calendar service for those interested in public relations, advertising, media, and marketing. When I first subscribed to Media Map in 1997, I received a monthly packet of disks that I had to install. It was a tedious chore that had to be repeated. Since then, EdCals.com has made its debut and has eliminated the extra work and hassle.

EdCals.com is an Internet-based search engine that brings together innovative Web technology with detailed media information from a research staff. The result is speedy access to an impressive array of publicity opportunities, plus in-depth intelligence on each story. In addition, those choosing to subscribe receive a personalized weekly e-mail bulletin listing all new and changed opportunities for one year, based on the topics, keywords, or publications the subscriber wants to monitor. Subscribers can search thousands of continuously updated editorial calendars that contain more than 100,000 upcoming stories and special issues from nearly every leading U.S. magazine and newspaper. One of the biggest benefits of the EdCals.com website is that you can obtain immediate results in just seconds.

NEWS WIRE SERVICES

There are two prominent contenders in the news wire services category: PR Newswire (www.prnewswire.com) and Business Wire (www.businesswire.com). Both services input, format, and electronically transmit news releases via satellite directly into the computer systems of local, regional, national, or global print, television, radio, consumer and business magazines, and wire services. News releases are electronically coded to reach the media circuit you have ordered. At your specified release time, an editor transmits your news release so it is received simultaneously by the media and, for disclosure purposes, received 15 minutes later by analysts and databases.

There are many circuits to choose from. National circuits in the United States provide the broadest U.S. media disclosure and cover most daily newspapers and broadcast outlets. Smaller U.S. geographic circuits enable you to target local media and are generally less expensive. Vertical targeted media circuits provide in-depth distribution to media covering a specific industry or theme. These vertical circuits can target the automotive, entertainment, financial services, health, and high-tech industries. With both companies, you get one or two circuits free. For those on a tight budget, it's cost-effective to select a small local circuit because of the widespread coverage you automatically receive through the free circuits.

Up until recently, I found sending a press release through the news wires to be a painstaking chore. First, I had to format it and send it to the newsroom electronically via e-mail. Then, I had to fax a hard copy. Last, I had to call the newsroom to ensure that they received the release through both communications methods. Fortunately, the Internet has simplified the process. Both services now have a secure site where you can upload press releases, photographs, or fax and e-mail lists. It's as simple as logging in with a password, specifying the date and time of the release, and attaching a file. Once sent, a wire service representative generally calls you to verify information. You receive a second courtesy call once the release has crossed the wires.

Both Business Wire and PR Newswire have expanded their offerings to include Web hosting, investor relations and archiving services, and broadcast faxing. Many startup companies and organizations with tight budgets consolidate their public relations, investor relations, and marketing needs through these two companies.

CYBER MEDIA TOURS

Cyber Media Tours (CMTs) are also growing in popularity. Companies (with large public relations budgets) often link a spokesperson via satellite (for video), their website (for content delivery and e-mail), and the telephone. Dell Computer Corporation and Medialink used a CMT to kick off a publicity campaign for CEO Michael Dell's book, *Direct from Dell: Strategies that Revolutionized an Industry*. The CMT featured industry icon Dell in a studio at the company's corporate headquarters in Round Rock, Texas, where he answered questions from selected television reporters and other journalists via both satellite and telephone connection. Questions had also been e-mailed from members of Dell's targeted press list. The event was digitized and streamed live over the Internet, where it was available to journalists and consumers alike.

This type of event provides further validation that media outlets are migrating to the Web. Industry experts believe journalists from the traditional media—television, radio, and print—are not just turning to the Internet for story ideas and information gathering; they are also using the Web as a medium through which they communicate with their sources.

OTHER WAYS TO REACH THE MEDIA

ProfNet

One of my favorite ways to use technology is through a service offered by PR Newswire called ProfNet. ProfNet is a subscription-based collaborative of public relations professionals linked by the Internet to give journalists and authors convenient access to expert sources. ProfNet states that it is a direct link to 6,000 news and information officers at colleges and universities, corporations, think tanks, national laboratories, medical centers, nonprofits, and PR agencies. For those trying to pitch the news media, it is touted as a central collection and distribution point for reporters' queries.

I have used ProfNet for several years and think it is the greatest thing since sliced bread. Several times a day, I receive an e-mail listing of stories that journalists and authors are working on. The categories of interest range from business to health, to computers, to law, to international affairs, to general interest. The yearly fee is under $2,000, which I think is well worth it if you are seeking free publicity.

The benefits of having a list of media opportunities delivered to you electronically are numerous. The reporters who post these queries need your help. They are searching for an expert, a source, or someone who is willing to be a case study. Generally, their deadlines are rapidly approaching and they have come to a brick wall. By responding to them with leads, regardless of whether the leads involve your company or are about people you know socially, you start building relationships. Later, you may find yourself pitching the reporter and your previous good will could pay off. I have often responded to queries about subjects that were not part of our usual media strategy. The end results were good, and I made some new media friends.

Technology will continue to drive competition in the news business. Technology speeds up the sense of urgency, and the luxuries of leisurely research are rapidly going by the wayside. Services like ProfNet will be instrumental in helping reporters fill their quotas of quality news seven days a week, 24 hours a day. Business Wire has followed this lead and created a similar service called ExpertSource, although it has yet to become as popular as ProfNet.

Video News Releases

Video news releases (VNRs) have become popular tools for securing publicity on television. VNRs are nothing more than 90 to 120 seconds of edited videotape, one or two sound bites (which are portions of a prerecorded interview), and a professional voiceover. In television broadcast news terms, a VNR is a "package." They are not commercials but actual news stories that have the same format, style, and quality that can be seamlessly integrated into a newsroom broadcast. To ensure optimal pickup, it's best to offer two versions of the VNR on the same videotape. One has the professional narration and the other has natural sound underneath all of the video except for the sound bites. Stations in smaller television markets tend to use the complete package, whereas newsrooms in larger markets may choose to have one of their reporters voice over the story. High-tech coding mechanisms can help you track the number of stations that air your VNR.

There has been great debate over the value of VNRs. If you have a VNR commercially produced, it can cost you more than $10,000, especially if a production crew has to go to multiple locations. The tracking services add to that expense. Finally, there is the cost to disseminate the videotapes to the television stations. The debate stems from how much VNRs are used in daily television news. From an industry standpoint, no formal research has been conducted on regular VNR usage by television stations. Chapter 9 includes some tips to reduce the costs of VNRs.

MARKETING AND PUBLICITY ON A SHOESTRING

The costs of marketing and public relations can be frightening, especially when you think about doing traditional radio, television, and print advertising or even hiring a public relations firm. In this day and age when the average price of a 30-second Super Bowl commercial runs close to $2 million, it's easy to see how some companies might set astronomical budgets to perform these tasks. And it's not just advertising; you may also need to have a hefty public relations budget. In California's Silicon Valley, it's common to find many public relations agencies that won't accept budgets or retainers lower than $20,000 per month. If you want their expertise, you'll have to come up with some big cash.

Having worked in these fields, I can tell you that it doesn't have to be like that. When I first started at Metricom, I had a budget of close to one-half million dollars. I worked with a public relations firm with a five-member team. We spent money like it was water. If I called one of the team members and talked for three or four minutes, I was billed for one-quarter of an hour. If a team member read an e-mail message I sent, I was billed for one-quarter of an hour. They even charged me for the time they spent figuring out my bill at the end of the month. Billing rates varied between $85 to $250 per hour, which was about average for Silicon Valley public relations agencies.

Needless to say, when my company started running short on funds, the public relations agency was the first to go. My budget was slashed from about $40,000 a month to $2,000 a month. The five-person agency team was gone, and actually, so was the entire Metricom corporate communications department. The only survivors were a young man named Dan Hubbard, who ran all of the marketing communications activities, and me—I was the "PR department." We were absorbed into the product-marketing group, which ultimately turned out to be the greatest thing that could happen to us because of the one-on-one communications with the product managers.

I think both Dan and I enjoyed the newfound freedom that comes when you are reclassified as an "individual contributor." The achievements Dan and I made in marketing and public relations that year were all ours. We found that the more ideas we came up with, the more work we made for ourselves, but it was great fun. We took pride in our achievements because they belonged solely to us. Dan, previously an underpaid and undervalued corporate communications "boy Friday," received a well-deserved promotion that year and a sizable increase in salary. My annual bonus was nice as well.

THINKING "OUT OF THE BOX"

By far the greatest accomplishment made by the two of us in our areas of expertise was being able to produce results on a shoestring budget. We had to come up with ideas that would have bottom-line impact, yet would cost only pennies. Let me tell you, it can be done. Neither Dan nor I had any money for advertising yet we had to make noise to sell modems. Shortly after the budget reductions, I devised a plan to go after all of the magazines that traditionally ran holiday gift guides or features on hot gadgets and gizmos. It was easy to find out who they were. I simply went on the Internet and looked up their websites.

I used part of my paltry budget to hire a friend of mine, Mary Babbitt, as a contractor for four hours a week. Mary had been a reporter and then anchor at one of the television stations where I had worked. She was the perfect person to help me pitch the media. She and I called the publications and tracked down the names of the editors who were spear-heading the gift guides. We pitched them—offering to send them demonstration units, photography, and whatever else they needed.

Our campaign worked like a charm. The wireless modem was featured in *Newsweek* that holiday season on the front page of a section entitled "Our Favorite Things." *Newsweek* even ran a color photograph of the modem attached to a Palm Pilot hand-held computer. In addition, the modem appeared on the cover of *ComputerEdge* magazine and in several popular high-tech industry publications. And, it was all free publicity. Not only did this national press coverage help us sell modems, but it also enabled us to produce some impressive, yet relatively inexpensive marketing collateral. We were able to reprint the articles and include them in sales and investor kits.

HOW MUCH WILL IT COST AND HOW MUCH CAN YOU AFFORD?

The first step in trying to do marketing and publicity activities on a shoestring budget is figuring out just what you'd like to accomplish. Do you want to create or increase brand awareness? Do you want to actually sell products and services? Do you want to increase your customer loyalty and retention? Do you want to change the perception of your company in the community? Setting an objective is critical to your success. It keeps you on track as you move toward achieving the objective, and it gives you a measurement tool at the end of the journey.

The next step is figuring out what you can do to meet your objective. With the holiday gift guide campaign, we knew we wanted to sell modems and increase brand awareness. We didn't have any money to spend on traditional advertising in newspapers and magazines, so we decided to take advantage of the editorial opportunities we knew existed. That was just one of the tactics we used to get the word out.

Finally, investigate the costs. Always be sure to ask if any costs are associated with supposedly "free" marketing and public relations opportunities. Fortunately, few publications subtly force you to advertise in order to receive news coverage. Radio, television, industry conferences, awards programs, the Web, and e-mail also offer many free and/or inexpensive ways to reach your objectives and accomplish your goals.

RESEARCH

As I mentioned previously, a wealth of free research is available through the Internet. Many companies and organizations offer summaries of their research and studies in the form of press releases, which they make available on their websites. Information written in press release form and distributed through commercial wire services is considered "public information," meaning that it can be used without obtaining permission from the author. If you reprint more than 250 words, however, it is wise to seek written permission.

For this book, I wanted to find out the latest statistics on information overload. I searched through all of the press releases on all of the professional industry research sites, such as GartnerGroup, IDG, the Yankee Group, and others. I reviewed news articles published by newspapers and magazines and made available online. I also did queries on websites, such as Ask Jeeves and Electronic Library. With all of this free data available, the Web has become an incredible source of information, which keeps expanding and getting richer every day.

Statistical Information

The number of websites that contain free statistical information continues to grow today and will become commonplace as the Web becomes the primary source for data in the coming years. eStats (www.estats.com) became a gold mine to me when I was "the corporate communications department" and had a limited budget. The site contains free marketing information, including new statistics on Internet usage, updates on e-commerce, and demographics on topics such as computer usage. The value of this kind of research to a marketer or publicity hound is indisputable.

Fun Quotations

I've often been successful at using the Web as a source for other free research. I have a personal fondness for putting memorable quotations into some of my marketing materials. They're easy to find. I simply type in the word "quotations" in my search engine, and presto—I have more websites with lists of quotations than I could possibly explore. In my searches, I even found a website that had quotations from leaders in the technology industry.

CUSTOMER RELATIONSHIP MANAGEMENT TOOLS

Much has been written about customer relationship management (CRM), which is characterized as technology-assisted selling. It helps companies manage the essential elements of making the first of many sales to a new customer and gives them the ability to keep existing customers satisfied. Companies today are realizing that they need CRM tools to help them go one step further to turn existing customers into long-term profits. The bottom line is that they want to increase customer satisfaction and retention while reducing costs. It's a huge challenge.

Toward the end of 1999, CRM was rapidly turning into electronic CRM (eCRM). Companies wanted to leverage the power of the Internet to communicate better with prospective and existing customers. By using the Internet, they could also reduce costs. According to AMR Research, Fortune 1000 organizations have accounted for most of the past growth in CRM. The research company believes, however, that the future of CRM growth actually lies with acceptance by small to mid-sized companies. For that to happen, out-of-the-box systems and solutions that require little customization must be provided. These products can be found through application service providers (ASPs).

An ASP is a Web-based business enterprise that does several things for its clients: (1) it hosts specific software applications; (2) it allows its subscribers to access the applications; (3) it stores related subscriber data and maintains the software and systems; and (4) it provides application individualization. One of the biggest benefits to using an ASP is that a company can get started with the service immediately and it's dependable.

The ASP is responsible for making sure everything works smoothly and reliably. The reliability can be compared to your telephone service. With the exception of natural disasters, it always works. Another benefit to using an ASP is that you have few upfront costs. You don't have to pay for equipment, installation, or extensive training.

◆ TECHNOLOGY THAT REDUCES THE HIGH COST OF LEADS

ContactMagic™, by NewEra (www.newera.com), is a simple, effective way to Web-enable CRM processes and improve marketplace integration. The CRM process has many different elements, but the bottom line is that all companies really want to do is to access important information, make critical phone calls, and complete tasks that are essential to them.

ContactMagic is a solution that can be implemented by people who are not college graduates, but who are generally energetic, bright, and enthusiastic people. They are trained in basic telemarketing for one to two weeks, instructed to deliver simple messages, and told how to effectively communicate to the people on the receiving line of the telephone. They use a software solution that is designed to run anyplace, anytime, and on any machine that has the Netscape browser or Internet Explorer.

"The cost of getting a sales professional on the street, actually selling your product, could run as high as a quarter of a million dollars when you factor in training, base salary, incentives, and time spent away from the pipeline attending corporate meetings and company functions," said Paul Robichaux, CEO of NewEra. "Their quotas, however, may be about half of that. Traditionally, sales people focus on one or two key prospects, work them, maybe get the sale and then have nothing in the pipeline. Our solution revolutionizes the whole process."

Robichaux's process utilizes people working at the low end of the sales chain and enables them to conduct high-volume, basic marketing with the goal of trying to generate prospects. The prospects can then be classified and moved up the sales chain. In the past, if the high-priced sales force managed the pipeline, then no one fed it at a lower level. This setup was particularly troublesome for small businesses.

With ContactMagic, telemarketers make the initial call and send out electronic information packages instead of traditional marketing collateral. These electronic packages are opened at an average rate of about 90 percent. At any point in time, a company can see the number of electronic packages that have been sent out and how many have been opened. The sales representative then knows exactly what is going on with each prospect.

The electronic packages all contain Web-based information using HTML. Marketing teams quickly realize they can eliminate the high costs associated with the creative development and actual production of collateral materials, such as brochures, product sheets, direct mail pieces, case studies, and so forth. In the past, these hard copy materials were also configured into a portable document format (PDF) and made available either through the Web or as an attached e-mail file. With the ContactMagic system, marketing teams are also able to eliminate the high cost of fulfillment, postage, and bad addresses. Updating is easy because it involves HTML and can be done whenever and wherever using the Web. NewEra estimates that it has reduced its own marketing collateral costs by about $11,000 per month, or $132,000 per year.

The value of this type of software solution is threefold. First, companies have better management of the contact management process, which enables them to hire telesales and telemarketing personnel at much lower cost levels. Second, the cost of their collateral design, production, and fulfillment could go to zero. Third, they have better tracking capabilities when it comes to unusual situations. With ContactMagic, they have the ability to escalate prospects and offer them a much higher level of quality responsiveness.

BANNER EXCHANGE NETWORKS

Banner exchange networks have been overlooked as one of the most important Internet applications for small websites. A banner exchange network is a medium that allows websites to swap banner advertising placements. Today, it is used by a growing number of Web-powered small and growing businesses to attract visitors. Because it is free, banner exchange is particularly effective for small companies without marketing and advertising budgets.

SmartAge.com (www.smartage.com) was the first of its kind to offer an automatically targeted, intelligent banner advertising service to small and growing businesses. Here's how it works: For every two banners that are displayed on your site for other SmartClicks' members, one of your banners is displayed on someone else's site. SmartClicks keeps the service free to you by selling the other banner ad display. SmartClicks also has Smart Targeting, which is intelligent software that learns where your ads perform better and responds to maximize your results. Whether you use SmartClicks or another banner exchange network, banner exchange is a proven way to drive traffic to websites, for free.

PRESS MATERIAL DEVELOPMENT AND DISTRIBUTION

The Crafting of a Press Release

It doesn't take an accredited public relations practitioner to write effective press materials. In fact, I would call most of it "formula writing." Take a press release, for example. Journalists want to know the "who, what, where, when, why, and how" of a story or event. They want just the facts—no hype or flowery adjectives. And they don't want to waste time reading long documents that either don't get to the point or repeat the point ad nauseum.

My philosophy for writing press releases is to keep them short and factual. If you review ten press releases written by ten different companies, you will definitely see a pattern in the way they are written. First, there's the headline, which is designed to capture the journalist's attention. If you don't grab them with the headline, then all effort is wasted. They won't read any further and your release will be relegated to the recycle bin.

The first paragraph should (and I say *should* because a lot of people do not do this) give journalists the "who, what, where, when, why, and how" of the story or event. If jour-nalists only read the headline and the opening paragraph, then they should have all the basic information they need. Journalists have often commented to me that they'd read the opening paragraph of a press release and wouldn't have any clue what it was about. I routinely see companies and indi-viduals use the opening paragraph of a press release to do their marketing. For example, "Mary Smith's company, a leading provider of the best homemade goodies on the planet, today announced that its chocolate-covered ant brownies, the chewiest and messiest dessert known to humankind, has been devoured by the president of the Chocolate Society." Forget the silliness of the content, this opening paragraph reads like a marketing brochure. I can almost guarantee that journalists worldwide would consider the release to be "a commercial" and toss it. So remember, just the facts please.

Back to the formula. The second paragraph is almost always a quote by someone, and that someone is usually (and preferably) a third party. Journalists rarely read quotes, and they seldom use them. At least with a third-party quote, you stand some chance of having it actually read.

The third paragraph is the meat of the release, including detail that explains or supplements the "who, what, where, when, why, and how." The fourth paragraph can do the same. Usually by the time journalists reach the fifth paragraph, press release writers have thrown in another quote, probably from a high-ranking executive of the organization. Again, the quote is rarely read and seldom used.

Once in awhile, you will find press releases that don't bother with quotes. I've met some investor relations professionals who refuse to put quotes in their financial press releases. I think that position is extremely smart because making statements that could be considered forward-looking or even some sort of hype designed to move the stock is risky in that business. Again, I like to keep press releases short, simple, and factual.

Send it Out: Press Material Distribution

Press releases can be distributed in many ways. For businesses and large organizations, the most popular way is to use one of the two large commercial wire services—PR Newswire or Business Wire. The fees vary depending on the length of your release and where you want it to go. If you want it to go to all news media organizations in the United States, for example, you would put it on a full national circuit. This circuit would include local, regional, and national newspapers and the satellite news-gathering offices of publications, wire services, and other electronic media, such as radio, television, and cable syndicated shows and stations. A press release that has national circuit distribution and is about 800 words in length can cost you more than $1,000.

The good news is that you can greatly reduce that expense. First of all, keeping your press release short and direct saves you money. Generally, if you exceed 400 words, you are charged by the addition of text, often in groups of 100 words. Also, you don't have to choose the national circuit. You may choose to send the release to a regional or even a local circuit, such as the San Francisco Bay area circuit. You now cut your cost by about two-thirds and still accomplish your disclosure and distribution goals. Plus, both commercial wire services throw in circuits, such as the trade publication and analyst circuits, for free. In the case of my high-tech company, we only really cared about the newspapers in our area, the analysts, and the trade publications.

Other cost-effective ways to distribute press releases involve a mix of the old and the new. You may want to send journalists your releases via e-mail, but I caution you to first check with them to find out if e-mail is their preferred method of delivery. You may also want to do broadcast faxing, which is a marvelous option found on most fax machines today that allows you to program a distribution list and start time. You can program the machine to send the release in the late evening or early morning hours when long-distance phone calls are less expensive. Finally, you can use the U.S. Postal Service, which is a fine distribution method if you have press releases that are "evergreen," meaning they don't have an expiration date. Use regular postal mail if there is no sense of urgency to get the releases into the hands of journalists. Examples include personnel announcements and feature press releases that may be accompanied by photographs.

◆ TELEVISION OPPORTUNITIES

Too often, people are intimidated by radio and television. They think the mediums are unapproachable and unfriendly. The reality is that most radio and television stations, especially those with news and public affairs department, rely on the public to fill airtime. Let's talk about television, a subject near and dear to my heart, first.

Television news offers endless opportunities to obtain exposure for your company, your product or service, or yourself. It's all free publicity through a visual communications vehicle that is extremely effective. How many times have you seen a person from a nonprofit organization talk about their cause on a live morning or afternoon news program? What about the retired military officer next door who is routinely asked to comment on national military issues?

How about the anchors and reporters who love to review and "demo" products and services as part of their consumer, health, or high-tech reports? My favorite example of free television publicity is when an anchor, reporter, or weatherperson chooses an event or backdrop to do their live reports. What a great opportunity to let the audience see what you are doing. Often, they will include an on-the-scene interview with you or someone in the organization.

Capturing the Attention of a Newsroom

Television news people tend to like faxes. The assignment desks in most TV newsrooms keep some sort of calendar/file in which they place faxes and hard copy information about upcoming events and story ideas. Usually at the end of the shift, the assignment editor will review the next day's file. The next morning, the editor makes recommendations to the producers about what stories and events should be covered. Most decisions about the day's news (not including breaking news) happen around 9 a.m. If you send a fax, then the chances are good that it will wind up in the file and be seen. A follow-up call is always a good reminder the night before your event or the morning of the event. Remember that television news programs have a lot of time to fill. Keep in mind that Sundays, Mondays, and holidays are generally hard to fill, and assignment editors may be in dire need of a good story.

Tips for Obtaining Television News Coverage

Most television stations that offer news programming have several shows each day. In most medium to large cities, they have a two-hour morning show, a 30-minute to one-hour noon show, a 5 p.m. show, a 6 p.m. show, and an 11 p.m. show. Each show has a producer. There is always a dayside assignment editor, and there is often a nightside person as well. They monitor breaking news and make recommendations for story and event coverage. Here are a few tips for obtaining television news coverage:

- Never call when a news program is on the air. During this time, all eyes in the newsroom are generally glued to television monitors that show the broadcasts of all three network affiliate stations in the market. In other words—your station and your competitors.

- Show meetings, which involve the assignment editor, the producer, the executive producer, and the news director, are generally held at 9 a.m. and 3 p.m. Do not call at these times because you won't be able to talk to any of the decision makers. It's okay to call before or after the show meetings, however, to find out if your story will be covered that day.

- Think about the video or pictures the audience will see before you pitch a story idea or event. Be prepared to offer a laundry list of video opportunities as part of your approach.

- Create a B-roll tape and make sure you let the news organization know you have one available. B-roll is video and natural sound of your product or subject. Having B-roll always increases your chances of coverage because it eliminates the need for television news crews to shoot the pictures themselves. It saves them time and energy.

- Don't think that having a politician or government official as part of your story will guarantee coverage. In fact, it can often work against you. Many journalists tend to shy away from these subjects because they don't want to give politicians a platform.

- Always promote the human angle of the story. Journalists from all mediums prefer to talk to ordinary people. For example, if a strike was held at an industrial plant, most journalists would approach the workers to learn first hand about how the strike affects them and their families, rather than asking company executives or representatives for their opinions.

Video

Producing a B-roll tape can be an expensive proposition, especially for a small business or nonprofit organization. If you hired a production company or a public relations firm to create one for you, it could cost you as much as $10,000 or more. There are, however, ways to get around these high costs and produce a tape that not only gets used by the media but also serves double duty on your website.

I have found that freelance videographers are available in almost every community. These can be people who work at the local television stations and are allowed to moonlight, former news shooters or corporate production people who have set up their own small operations, or freelancers who work for network affiliate news bureaus, such as CNN. I have often called the CNN offices in my city and asked for a list of freelancers who either own their own equipment or can rent it.

The day rate for a freelance videographer is approximately $1,200. I think they provide a great value because they absorb the cost of the equipment (which is expensive) and are generally news professionals. They know how to shoot in a news style, which is extremely important if you want the tape to be used by TV stations. They are also fast. Unlike commercial production companies, they are trained to set up quickly, get the shots they need, and move on to the next location. Always ask them to shoot on Beta because that is the common format for news.

The next step is to get your tape edited. The videographer can often either do the job personally or recommend another freelancer or editing facility. You will usually be charged an hourly rate for the editing session plus the cost of the tape. You will want to keep each shot to about 10 to 15 seconds in length so that the television stations have plenty to work with when they edit their stories. You'll want to have at least one-half dozen Beta copies on hand to give out. You may also want to use the video on your website, so consider getting several VHS dubs of the finished edited B-roll for that purpose.

RADIO OPPORTUNITIES

Radio stations offer a wide variety of free publicity opportunities as well, including news programs, public service announcements, talk shows, special promotions, and give-aways. There are many ways to have fun and to accomplish your marketing and publicity goals.

News

Whether a radio station does 24-hour news or just hourly newscasts, the reporters and anchors need to fill time. The stories are usually short. They are also localized, so if you live or work in a community, the radio news staff is more open to your story ideas and events. One thing to remember about radio is that although it is not a visual medium, reporters still have to tell a story by making it come alive for the listener.

In 1993, I made the transition from television news to CBS radio. I was anchoring live coverage of the Space Shuttle launches from the Kennedy Space Center, in Florida. In my little studio, which was located approximately three miles from the launch pad, I hung signs everywhere that read "Say what you see." I needed to use my words to describe the event to the audience. Today, you need to remember that visual stories are good for radio as well as television, and that reporters often use their words and the natural sound of the activities going on around to tell the story.

Talk Shows

With talk radio, producers generally have one to three hours to fill with special guests, experts, politicians, and other interesting people. These shows are great if you or someone from your organization has expertise in a particular area. Sometimes producers ask people with different or opposing views on issues to participate in a debate. Other times, representatives from nonprofit groups are asked to appear on a show to give in-depth information about a particular subject, cause, or activity. I have even heard rock-and-roll radio announcers invite authors to chat on their shows about the books they've written. Finally, a growing number of consumer-oriented shows ask guests to appear to talk about new products, services, or industry trends. These opportunities can be secured with a mere phone call and some background material.

Some of the secrets to becoming a "regular" or repeat guest on these types of shows include making yourself available at a moment's notice, building a relationship with the producers, and establishing a reputation as an interesting, knowledgeable, enthusiastic, and articulate guest.

Another important tip to remember when pitching a radio talk show is that you need to be familiar with the program on which you want to appear. This involves listening to the show every day for one week or more. You want to get a feel for the type of guests who appear, the type of issues and topics covered, and the host's broadcast style. You want to be well prepared before you pick up the telephone. You may also want to call the station and ask if the show has a producer, a guest "booker," or if the host does all of the planning and scheduling.

Public Service Announcements

Radio stations across the country have a never-ending challenge to secure the maximum amount of advertising possible. More advertising means more revenue—it's pretty simple. Unfortunately, competition is stiff and some radio stations find themselves with large blocks of time—in the late evening and early morning hours—in which they have no commercials. The radio announcers feel they must talk about something other than the names of the songs and the weather. That is where free public service announcements (PSAs) come into play.

PSAs are exactly what they sound like. They are announcements about activities and events going on in the community, usually by nonprofit organizations or companies that have nothing monetary to gain. PSAs are usually about 15 to 30 seconds long and are read, verbatim, by the announcer. The easiest way to get your PSA aired is to write down the "who, what, where, when, why, and how" on a piece of paper and put it in the mail. Radio stations continually rotate the announcements, so yours will most likely get aired. Of course, the fewer announcements the station has at a given point in time, the more yours gets read.

A few tips about public service announcements: (1) Always keep them short, but be sure to include all of the pertinent information. (2) Always include a phone number. It's also great to have a live person ready to answer the phone, or at least have an answering machine on standby. (If you motivate people to call and then frustrate them, your efforts have been wasted.) (3) Don't forget the Web. If you have a website, be sure to include the URL, or Web address, when you send the information. (4) Last, you may also want to call the station before you mail the announcement information to find out who is responsible for writing and running PSAs. Sometimes the station has a public service or community services director, but the job often falls on the news department or a clerical person.

Special Promotions and Give-Aways

One of the most successful ways to get free publicity on the radio involves giving away free stuff. Almost all radio stations have a promotions director who is responsible for obtaining prizes, orchestrating give-aways, and setting up special promotional events. Almost every day and sometimes every hour, a radio announcer runs a contest in which listeners call in to win something. In addition, they'll often go to a location where something really cool is happening, broadcast live on-the-scene, and give away free stuff. The beauty of the give-away is that the announcers chat about the product or service on-air, which is great promotion for you. They may even invite you to broadcast live with them, which is a perfect opportunity for you to tout your goods. Last, with the arrival of the Web, you have the added bonus of being recognized online as well. It's so easy today for radio stations to list sponsors, feature logos, and show actual photographs of the things they are giving away.

LINKING

Having your website hyperlinked to other sites can be extremely valuable for building brand awareness and increasing your chance of e-commerce success. The dictionary definition of a link is something that connects two objects. That is exactly what a hyperlink does. It links two Web pages together and makes it easy for the computer user to make the move from one to another. For example, if you were an author like me, you'd want to have a hyperlink on your promotional website that takes visitors to one of the large online bookstores, such as www.amazon.com or www.barnesandnoble.com, so they can easily purchase your books. On the flip side, I'd want my website designer to have a link to my Sierra Communications public relations site, which would not only build brand awareness for me but also serve as a real-world example of his talent for him.

The key to creating a successful linking campaign goes back to a person or company's ability to build relationships and provide value. The linking agreement often has to benefit both parties in some way. A graphic design firm may let you use its funny cartoon characters on your website in exchange for a link to its site. An online entertainment guide may provide a link to your limousine service in exchange for complementary promotion in your print ads. The possibilities are endless if you can offer a mutually beneficial relationship.

MIXING TECHNOLOGY WITH TRADITION

Technology has undeniably changed the face of marketing and public relations in the latter part of the twentieth century. When I joined McDonnell Douglas Aerospace at the Kennedy Space Center in Florida in 1994, I hadn't even heard of the Internet. I remember one of our computer guys showing me a marvelous thing on his PC screen—Mosiac.

Mosaic was the first graphical Web browser. Two young men, Marc Andreesen and Eric Bina, created it while they were working at the National Center for Supercomputing Applications (NCSA) at the University of Illinois. Posted on the Internet, it was free to all. It later evolved into what we now know today as Netscape Navigator.

The Internet and the World Wide Web put online research at my fingertips. It also opened up a whole new way for me to communicate with internal and external audiences. As I became more technologically savvy, I also started to realize that you couldn't depend on just technology alone. I needed to find the perfect mix of technology and tradition.

KNOW YOUR TARGET AUDIENCE AND SET YOUR BUSINESS OBJECTIVES

One of the biggest mistakes in marketing today is not knowing who you are trying to influence or what your objectives are. The Internet, the World Wide Web, e-mail, and some of the other technologies mentioned in this book give us the ability to communicate with millions of people. Without researching your target audience or setting objectives upfront, your efforts can be for naught. Many companies today build their websites without thinking about branding, consistent messaging, or continuity with their printed collateral. As a result, their marketing efforts are ineffective and they waste a considerable amount of time and money. Remember the definition of marketing: *The matching of products or services to the needs of consumers as discovered through research of things such as their attitudes, opinions, and behavior.*

Know your audience. The key here is traditional research. You may want to use technology to help you with e-mail questionnaires or online surveys. You can commission organizations such as Harris Interactive, which is the world leader in Internet-based market research and polling, to help you with quick polls. Or, you may choose to do informal research such as personal contact (person-on-the-street-interviews), community forums, and advisory committees.

Set your objectives. Objectives are specific milestones that measure progress toward the achievement of a goal. They require a designated level of accomplishment, a time frame in which the accomplishments are to occur, a target audience, and the desired result. I try to set objectives for every marketing and public relations project I undertake. They help me stay focused while I'm working on the project. When I'm finished, they serve as a great tool for measuring my success. At the end of the day, it's all about measurable results.

INFORMATION OVERLOAD

According to a 1996 study by the Institute for the Future, Pitney Bowes, and the Gallup Organization, the myth of technology is that it replaces old tools with more efficient new ones. The study claims that, in reality, technology tools are layered on top of older tools. We can see that clearly by looking at all of the communications technologies that are available today. We have the phone, cellular phones, voice mail, e-mail, faxes, pagers, hand-held computers, laptop computers, the U.S. Postal Service, and overnight delivery services. All of these communications tools involve truly a mix of the old and the new.

In 1999, Pitney Bowes followed up with another study that looked at office workers, technology, and the information overload phenomenon. Results showed that office workers received an average of 201 messages per day via one form of technology or another. Information overload had arrived.

ABUSING TECHNOLOGY

As the twentieth century drew to a close, probably the most well-known abuse of technology was related to e-mail. According to many of the computing dictionaries on the market today, *spam* is unsolicited bulk e-mail sent via the Internet. Another way to spam people is through USEnet newsgroup postings that are sent to large numbers of newsgroups.

Spamdexing

Spamdexing is a new form of abuse used by some Web marketers and hosts as a way of keeping their services at the top of search engine results. Spamdexing includes submitting multiple, yet slightly altered, websites to a search engine, and "word stuffing," which places a word or keywords in a site numerous times, to ensure that the search engine will bring up the site as one of the top keyword matches. Other techniques include "bait-and-switch" gimmicks, such as loading the site with commonly used (and attention-grabbing) keywords such as "free," "sex," "money," or "shareware," even though the words are not related to the actual site content.

News Wire Hoaxes

News wires have also been the targets of abuse and hoaxes. On April 26, 1999, Business Wire filed a lawsuit in federal court against three perpetrators of a recent online hoax who used Business Wire's press release distribution services to publicize a phony investment opportunity. The defendants submitted a press release to Business Wire on behalf of a company called "Webnode" announcing that the U.S. Department of Energy (DOE) had granted Webnode an exclusive contract to raise funding for the Next Generation Internet (NGI). Although the NGI is a bona fide project, Webnode—and its supposed contract with the government—is a sham. The bogus press release also included a fake solicitation for investments and directed readers to the Webnode.com website where they could register to invest.

The defendants responded to inquiries about Webnode and collected personal information from nearly 2,000 people who believed, based on information in the phony press release, that they had a genuine opportunity to get in on the ground floor of the NGI, the lawsuit alleges. Based on the Webnode crew's assurances that the press release was genuine, Business Wire distributed the news over its wire service and posted it on the businesswire.com website. The defendants' false announcement, with the Business Wire trademark prominently displayed on the byline, was made available to millions of readers. Business Wire's lawsuit alleged violations of federal and state trademark laws, fraud, breach of contract, defamation, and conspiracy and sought unspecified damages and injunctive relief.

Copy Cats

Another example of an abuse of technology for competitive gain put Yahoo!, the first online navigational guide to the Web, in the victim's seat. In spring of 1999, Yahoo! filed suit against two companies that they believe forged the headers of thousands of promotional e-mail messages to look as though they came from yahoo.com addresses. They alleged it was a major spam campaign that not only caused harm to Yahoo!'s reputation with consumers but also forced Yahoo! to dedicate a large amount of resources to handle the complaints and returned messages.

Voice Mail Commercials

By mid-1999, another extremely annoying abuse of technology had surfaced, this time using answering machines and voice mail. I'll never forget the day I came home and checked my voice mail, only to find that a computer had left a "commercial" on my machine. It lasted several minutes, and because I had an older-generation answering machine, I had no choice but to let it run its course. At the end of the message, I was given a toll-free telephone number. I called, but still no human being was available. It was (surprise, surprise) an answering machine that gave me yet another lengthy commercial. At the end, it asked me to leave my name and telephone number and a "representative" would get back to me. No traceable information was provided through any of these communications methods. I still can't tell you today what the name of the company is because I never talked to a real person.

The best advice I can give to marketers and those interested in free publicity is to put themselves in the target audience's shoes. How would you feel if you were the recipient of an unsolicited, questionable e-mail or voice-mail message? How would you feel if your search engine took you to a website that had absolutely nothing to do with the subject in which you were interested? Or if you were enjoying a newsgroup and some weird, totally inappropriate, irrelevant commercial message came across? I call this my "Do unto others" marketing philosophy. Be smart about the communications you send.

THE HUMAN TOUCH

The successful marketer and public relations practitioner of tomorrow will use a blend of technology and tradition to be successful. You can use some of the newer tools and techniques listed in this book to effectively reach and influence your target markets, but you will also need to combine them with some of the old tools and techniques of the past.

When talking about marketing on websites, a popular industry phrase used often is "stickiness." Stickiness refers to the length of time a person stays on a site, which equates into the opportunity you have to capture their interest and influence them in the way you desire. Stickiness is good, but making a sale or achieving your public relations or marketing goal is better.

Today you can purchase almost anything online. It's easy to plan a vacation, order consumer products, send flowers, purchase life insurance, or even buy a car online. It's as simple as finding the proper website, filling out an online form, and hitting the submit button. Tomorrow, with technology like proactive portals and Push technology, the process will become even easier. You won't have to search for what you want or need; the opportunity will miraculously come to you.

It is rapidly becoming apparent, however, that the one missing ingredient in performing these online transactions is the human touch. In the summer of 1999, Allstate Insurance ran an extensive radio and television campaign that I thought was effective. The television commercial showed complete devastation of a neighborhood following a tornado. Homes were reduced to boards and timber, remnants of lives were strewn about the ground, and families were hugging and crying and clearly suffering from their losses. An Allstate Insurance claims adjuster walked into the on-screen picture, offering a family the one thing online insurance brokers cannot—the human touch. He was offering comfort, personal service and support, and empathy. The tag line was brilliant—"You're in good hands, mine."

The Allstate website complements its traditional radio and television advertising campaign. It sports a new customer care service feature as well as a hot button that takes you to its catastrophe information center. There is a "safety matters" section as well as an "in the community" section. Through an integrated marketing campaign, Allstate is clearly sending the message that it's a company that cares.

More One-To-One Communication

No one argues that companies doing business online must do everything they can to preserve their existing customers. Carlson Leisure Group—a world leader in leisure travel and travel agency franchising—has a website where customers can go to make online travel plans. However, Carlson also uses Push technology software to deliver critical business information to its more than 10,000 travel agents worldwide. Carlson uses Push software to notify agents of market changes through attention-grabbing "flashes," or customized multimedia alerts, that are delivered to the sales force regardless of the application currently running. The priority of each flash is tiered according to importance. They cannot be ignored like faxes and e-mail.

Through this targeted delivery of specialized information, the technology assists Carlson's leisure and franchise agencies in becoming consumer advocates. For example, a travel franchise or individual agent may receive notice (via a flash) about airline seats, hotel rooms, or car rental promotions that are about to expire. They then make personal calls to their clients who have expressed interest previously in certain travel destinations. They pass on information about what could now be considered a super bargain. Although the client may not be in a position to accept the great offer, chances are good that the client will remember the personalized customer service provided to them by the agent. The relationship will be enhanced and strengthened. As a result, customers may continue to opt for personalized service instead of simply using a website when booking their travel. By marketing to customers on a one-to-one basis, Carlson has the opportunity to build lifetime value and retention.

Fast Response Times

It's also important to remember the little things when dealing with people, whether you're using technology or your own personal skills. One of the key factors to achieving business success in the next century will be the ability to respond quickly. As technology helps us become more efficient, we also become further removed from our customers. How many times have you gone to a website and been unable to find a phone number of a company or individual? You're forced to rely on the e-mail address they provide. So you send off an e-mail message and never hear a word back. It happens all the time. Or perhaps you've sent a question into a company's technical support unit. You receive an instant return message acknowledging receipt of your message, but again, you wait interminably for a response that never comes.

One of my friends, a young woman named Julie Rowinski, works in the investor relations department of a newly public company. One day she was surprised to read a message on the Yahoo! financial page about her. An investor posted a nice message, complimenting her and her company for the quick response to an inquiry. Her personal work ethic was one in which she always returned phone calls and e-mail messages as soon as she could and always tried to help the company's investors get the information they needed. Apparently she was a bit of an exception in Silicon Valley for both investor relations and public relations.

When dealing with the news media, my philosophy is similar. I always call journalists back immediately because they are probably on deadline and need answers quickly. I treat all journalists with the same level of interest as well. It's been my experience that the technology reporter working at the *Santa Maria Times* may one day become a bureau chief for the *Wall Street Journal*. It happens all the time. I also pay attention to their needs during the interview process. If they need artwork, I have it delivered through an overnight service. I try to meet their needs immediately, and it pays off. If they are successful in what they do, then I have taken another step toward strengthening my relationship with them.

Customer Care

I applaud the companies that have seemingly realized the importance of "customer care." Several years ago, I worked with a telemarketing group called Business Tel (www.businesstel.com), which is located in San Jose, California. Business Tel was touted as a market leader in developing and executing customer acquisition programs as well as helping companies with customer retention. I know they had great success in acquiring customers because their website boasts that they took one client from $26 million to $62 million in sales in just 18 months. What really impressed me, however, was their ability to interact with customers once they made a purchase. Business Tel had one young woman, Melissa Butz, who called existing customers all day long just to check to see how they were doing with the product and its complimentary service. Her efforts prevented dozens of customers from dropping the service and returning the product. She truly took care of the customer, and her company maintained a competitive edge.

The Thank You Note

Finally, one of my favorite relationship-building techniques does not involve e-mail or voice mail or any other technology. It involves a sheet of paper and a pen. I'm talking about the traditional thank you note. By the time I was old enough to write my own name, my mother had me writing thank you notes. If I received Christmas presents from grandparents, aunts, and uncles, I had to write my thank you notes and get them mailed before January first. It wasn't something that I liked to do, but today, I can't thank my mom enough for making me do it. Today, my children are following suit.

In business, the thank you note is almost a thing of the past. I can't remember when I last received one. Whenever I start a new job, the first thing I do is to order blank notecards with the company's logo on the front. I send thank you notes out like crazy. I send them to customers for serving as references for the news media. I send them to the news media for writing accurate and fair stories. I send them to the senior executives' administrative assistants after they have completed logistically grueling tasks. I send them to my co-workers for helping me out when I'm in a pinch. I firmly believe that you can help make a mark for yourself or your company by simply writing thank you notes. You certainly will stand out in a crowd because nobody else seems to bother to make this simple gesture of good will.

PUBLICITY STUNTS

As the need to garner publicity about products and services becomes more intense, you'll soon find companies following an effective trend in marketing called *marketing-based public relations*. Over the last few years, we have seen companies such as Volkswagen and Gillette begin their marketing efforts with public relations campaigns and publicity stunts. In the case of Volkswagen, the company used a mix of technology and tradition to debut the new Bug. It provided sneak peeks over the Internet as well as through more traditional venues such as car shows. Prelaunch events eventually translated into record-breaking sales for the Bug even before the car was available to the general public. Through prelaunch public relations and promotional activities, Gilette was able to build a market share for its new Mach 3 razor of more than 30 percent.

CASE STUDY: PIZZA A GO GO, PIZZA MY HEART

Chuck Hammers is a master of publicity. He has routinely been able to get his four pizza restaurants covered by the news media and into the public eye by using relatively low-cost special events and publicity stunts. His first media adventure involved the purchase of a Humvee. A Humvee is actually a high-mobility multi-purpose wheeled vehicle (HMMWV) that was designed for the U.S. Army. Humvees were made available to civilians in 1991, and Hammers thought it would be an unusual way to deliver pizza. His big idea, according to his wife, Mary, was to use it for big deliveries like to summer camps at Stanford University or arts and wine festivals.

Soon, Hammers' Humvee began to garner some media attention. It first began with Smithsonian magazine, which was doing an article on pizza in America. The magazine wanted to include a section on the San Francisco Bay area, and as the story goes, heard about the Humvee. Hammers was featured in a photograph that had him leaning against the Humvee holding a pizza. The side of the Humvee said "The Ultimate Delivery Machine."

From there, the *San Francisco Examiner* did a story, and then the San Francisco network-affiliate television stations did features. The Associate Press eventually caught wind of it and then CNN. The story happened to catch the media's attention on one of those days when there wasn't much breaking news. It was also an extremely unique and visual story. Everyone loved the idea of having their pizza delivered in a Humvee, so everyone covered it. Because it hit the Associated Press news wire, the story was sent all over the country. Hammers could not have asked for better free publicity.

Hammers' next success story involved the San Jose Sharks, a National Hockey League team, that was popular in the San Francisco Bay area. Since Hammers' flagship restaurant was located in downtown San Jose, close to the basketball arena, he thought it might be fun to use large aquariums as part of his decor. Of course, he put two small sharks in the tanks. After all, the San Jose Sharks' team mascot was a shark. What could be more appropriate?

When the San Jose Sharks made it to the playoffs, Hammers had even more fun with his sharks and received more media attention. He would name the fish that were going to be food for his pets after the opposing team's star players. Television stations loved it. Then, one night, Sharkey, the hockey team's giant blue mascot, got caught in the rafters of the arena while making his entrance. Comedy Central, the comedy television channel, did a story on Sharkey getting stuck in the rafters and used Pizza A Go Go as the backdrop. Again, Hammers garnered widespread publicity for his restaurant.

Hammers realized early on that people have many choices for food, especially pizza. He figured that he needed to make the act of going to his restaurant an event. He refers to it as "event-oriented dining." Through all of the positive national media coverage, his restaurant became known as "the place that has the Humvee" and "the place that has the sharks." You can bet that when the media needs to quickly find a Humvee or a shark tank, they'll be knocking on Pizza A Go Go's door.

TOLL-FREE PHONE NUMBERS

Believe it or not, in some cases, functions such as technical support are no longer free. Big companies, such as Microsoft Corporation, are not only making customers pay toll charges for technical support calls, but in some cases they also have to pay for Web or telephone "assisted personal support." In the future, companies that continue to offer toll-free, no-charge assisted support will have a competitive edge. Customers value the ability to talk to a tech-support professional toll free. After all, they paid for the product or service. Do they have to pay to learn how to use it as well? This "paid assisted support" reminds me of the aforemetioned public relations agency I once worked with that charged me to tabulate my monthly bill. In the end, consumers will not tolerate these activities and will begin to wield more power with their money.

GOING ABOVE AND BEYOND THE CONSUMER'S OBVIOUS NEEDS

I have seen several companies master the art of going above and beyond in order to meet the needs of their customers and potential customers. Their secret is that they proactively make information available. I think Amazon.com is the first good example. When I log in, the website knows who I am and what I've purchased before. It knows my interests and tastes. It uses my personal profile and history and a database of millions of books to suggest new reading material. It goes above and beyond by saving me time and providing value.

Another company that goes the extra mile to provide value to its customers is Texas Instruments. Its website offers a large library of technology tools and information for semiconductor and electronic engineers. By providing this useful information, they're helping people do their jobs better. They're also providing a valuable service and subtly promoting their products. The engineers who visit and use this site will most likely tell their co-workers and counterparts in the industry. Texas Instruments stands to benefit from increased customer satisfaction and word-of-mouth advertising.

WHAT'S NEXT?
THE PROS TALK
ABOUT TODAY
AND TOMORROW

When you start a project like developing a public relations campaign, implementing a marketing plan, or even writing a book, it's important to get input from professionals in different fields. They can provide you with a totally different perspective on what you are doing, or they can enhance your project by providing you with fresh ideas and suggestions.

So I asked my peers in various professions to offer personal insight

---

CASE STUDY: USING TECHNOLOGY TO BRING SHAMU TO YOU—PR WITH A PORPOISE

Written by Bob Tucker, director of public relations for SeaWorld San Diego since 1998. He has also served in various high-level public relations positions for Boeing and Rockwell, and he is a 10-year veteran of television news reporting.

In the highly competitive theme park industry, success depends on the number of guests being driven through the turnstiles each day. In fact, at most parks, daily attendance is so important that hourly counts are often fed into the pagers of senior management so they can constantly track the numbers.

At SeaWorld in San Diego, public relations plays a vital role in the marketing mix to attract guests. Public awareness is kept high through successful pitches to news reporters that result in key newspaper placements and visibility on local television. Not only is it the unique subject matter—marine mammals, fish, and birds—that distinguish SeaWorld story pitches from most others, but it is also the park's technology capabilities.

With Betacam cameras and editing systems, SeaWorld's Emmy Award–winning video team provides the production quality and standards TV stations expect. Outfitted with a direct microwave link to all four San Diego TV stations, SeaWorld videographers shoot, edit, and feed video several times a week. Nearly all of the material makes it on the air. For stations desiring live broadcasts, SeaWorld owns a multi-camera microwave truck that can be set up at any location throughout the 189-acre park. Fiberoptic cable has been installed in many areas, making just about any location "camera ready."

During special events, the high-tech envelope is pushed even further. In May 1999, SeaWorld unveiled its newest attraction, a water ride named "Shipwreck Rapids." During the week leading up to the ride's grand opening, TV reporters were invited to ride Shipwreck Rapids and utilize "castaway cam." Positioned on a raft, the camera provided viewers with an up-close and first-hand look at the reporter's reactions during the three-minute splashy ride. The entire waterway was equipped with transmitting devices enabling reporters to provide an uninterrupted live broadcast during the entire ride. Stations in Los Angeles, San Diego, Palm Springs, Phoenix, and Tucson sent reporters who used "castaway cam" to promote Shipwreck Rapids to thousands of people in each market.

Another high-tech adventure awaiting TV reporters at SeaWorld is a rare opportunity to "swim with the sharks." Using SeaWorld's underwater camera, and a wireless microphone, reporters can plunge into the Shark Encounter exhibit. Surrounded by hammerheads, white tips, and dozens of other sharks, reporters can go "live" inside the exhibit's 280,000-gallon tank and interview experts about the fascinating world of sharks. It's something viewers really eat up.

As for national TV coverage, the SeaWorld PR team often uplinks VNRs and B-roll as part of the Zoo News Network, a weekly satellite feed to TV stations throughout the nation. The video, which usually features a fuzzy, furry animal or cute and cuddly marine mammal, appears during the last 30 seconds of a newscast, leaving viewers with a warm, uplifting feeling.

SeaWorld's toolbox of high-tech PR devices is not just reserved for broadcast reporters. The park also works with print publications in several ways. Probably the most common SeaWorld PR placements in major newspapers and weekly magazines are photos of celebrity visits. The park's photo team snaps shots of celebrities posing with a whale, dolphin, or some other SeaWorld friend. With the celebrity's approval, the finished product is then electronically sent to wire services and entertainment magazines that often print them in upcoming editions. Celebrities visiting the park during the summer of 1999 included Bob Hope, Geena Davis, Diane Keaton, sports stars, and several well-known musicians. The park's photo team also produces digitally enhanced images. Commonly used in advertising, brochures, and other marketing materials, the images are created in-house, saving time and money.

SeaWorld's PR team is armed with digital pagers, cell phones, voice mail, blast fax machines, and other high-tech tools of the trade. In the fast-paced world of newsgathering, the PR team's goal is to respond rapidly, helping facilitate the coverage needs of reporters. With that kind of proactive philosophy, there's no doubt the positive relationship between SeaWorld and the news media will continue to go swimmingly for years to come.

CASE STUDY: TECHNOLOGY—NO FAIR WEATHER FRIEND IN TELEVISION NEWS

Written by Jim Barach, chief meteorologist at WTVH-TV, a 20-year veteran of television news who has forecast the weather for stations across the country since 1980. He has also received the television seal of approval from both the National Weather Association and the American Meteorological Society.

In prehistoric times, that means before the History Channel, news was spread across the land by drums, or by the town crier. However, these methods were slow, and were hard to sell commercial time on, so television was invented. Besides wiping out "tom tom elbow" and many cases of laryngitis, television brought world events right into living rooms, bedrooms, and sports bars across the country. But even though television was the greatest invention in the history of humankind, some people felt it could actually be made better.

Spurred on by the technology revolution (and the fact that television stations had way too much money), more and more gadgets were introduced to capitalize on the ever-shrinking attention span of the American viewing public. Of all these, the most overused and abused, loved and hated, and criticized news element—besides, of course, the wisecracking sports guy—is "the live eye," "the live remote," "the live shiny van," or whatever slick name your station chose to use to overmarket and overexploit its virtues.

The first live remote broadcast I ever did was in 1980 in Farmington, New Mexico. If you are looking on a map, it's not near anything. We thought it was a technological breakthrough just to *have* television in Farmington, but the presidential election was coming up and we were determined to have the local political celebrations live! It took a team of four engineers one week of working around the clock, cannibalizing every coat hanger and hubcap lying around the station to try to bounce a microwave signal in from about three-and-a-half miles down the road. Even so, it was the biggest technological breakthrough in New Mexico since the people of Lincoln County were warned about Billy the Kid by telegraph.

Live remotes were originally used to show actual news that was happening at that very moment. But then it was realized that it could also be used to get the smart-aleck weather guy that nobody likes out of the station to talk about the weather somewhere else, preferably far away. Sometimes it wasn't far enough, so satellite technology was invented. Even as I write this I am flying back from covering Hurricane Floyd. My station flew me 1,200 miles so I could try to stand on a pier in South Carolina and be whipped by 100-mph winds in order to tell the folks back home, in Syracuse, that I was doing something very stupid, LIVE! Satellite trucks were parked every 30 feet from Florida to North Carolina. All we had to do was give the satellite people an ungodly sum of money and presto—my mug was beamed all over the world to be picked up by anyone with a satellite dish and the spare time to flip through 822 channels.

But technology hasn't stopped there. Computers have also worked their way into the weather department. After a half century of TV news it was finally discovered that the only reason anyone watches news at all is to get tomorrow's forecast. Personalized Doppler radar, lightning detectors, and "storm trackers" are all a "must have" for every weather weenie worth their bowtie. "Street level mapping" lets a meteorologist alert the people living at Fifth and Vermont to make sure they put their insurance premium in the mail in the next 5 minutes before they are leveled by an F-4 tornado. Computers don't make us any more accurate, but at least they make some pretty graphics to help explain what happened to yesterday's forecast.

The Internet is becoming a newsroom staple. It can be a source of information on virtually any subject (except the one you are assigned), and of course used to e-mail resumes around the nation with only the touch of a button. Yes, technology is changing the business of broadcasting and will continue to do so. In fact, it's changing so fast that by the time you read this I will be obsolete. See you in the TV Museum.

CASE STUDY: INVESTOR RELATIONS AND THE INTERNET

Written by Deborah Demer, who founded Demer IR Counsel, Inc. in 1989, after 10 years in corporate investor relations. In addition to her lengthy career, she has served as an adjunct instructor of Investor Relations at Golden Gate University, in San Francisco, which is the only graduate-level investor relations course of its kind on the West Coast.

Like many other information-driven business disciplines, investor relations (IR) is being transformed by the Internet. According to Forrester Research, the aggregate value of all online trading accounts is expected to grow from approximately $350 billion today to more than $3 trillion in 2003. Jupiter Communications estimates that online trading constitutes 14 percent of all securities transactions and 30 percent of retail transactions today. As a result, IR has never played a more important role in the financial industry.

Historically, corporate IR has targeted the institutional investment community, or *buy side*, and the investment banking, brokerage, and research firms that have served it, or *sell side*. Make no mistake, this universe continues to drive market valuations. However, the democracy of the Internet also gives individual investors instantaneous access to an explosion of news and information. For the first time, individual investors have the ability to execute their own trades. Their impact on the stock market has propelled the Dow Jones, Standard & Poor, Nasdaq, and other major indices to record levels, while creating unprecedented volatility.

In addition, the New York Stock Exchange and Nasdaq have publicized plans to extend their trading hours for the benefit of individual and institutional investors. Sophisticated electronic communications networks (ECNs) enabling after-hours trading, once the exclusive venue of institutional investors, are becoming increasingly accessible to individuals. The prospect of 24-hour, seven-day trading for the masses is no longer a futuristic fantasy.

As a result, IR is evolving to encompass the retail investment community—largely where the traditional retail infrastructure of stockbroker and floor trader have disappeared—in addition to the powerful institutional audience. As far as the corporate IR practitioner is concerned, the Internet is both cause and effect. Just as the Web enabled this trend, so can the Web be used to feed it. Here are some practical implications and applications of Internet technology for those interested in investor relations:

- The challenge of material disclosure and market reaction. Imagine releasing quarterly financial results that are either above or below Wall Street expectations *during market hours*-because the premarket and after-market windows for investor digestion of the news have virtually closed. This requires significantly higher levels of sensitivity in news release drafting and distribution to a proliferation of online news sources, as well as a rethinking of strategies and tactics for managing expectations through guidance and preempting surprises.

- Internet broadcast e-mail is replacing mailings and broadcast faxes as the news distribution medium of choice, particularly among institutions. Reflexively, e-mail notification services alert investors to special events such as corporate announcements, SEC filings and stock conference appearances.

- The complexity and sophistication of IR websites is increasing exponentially to meet the information needs of a broad range of investors. In addition to news releases, annual reports, stock quotes, and frequently asked questions, these sites include more detailed food for analysis, such as historical stock price trends and valuation ratios.

- The more advanced IR sites also include Webcasts of quarterly results teleconferences, intra-quarter management updates (a.k.a. "fireside chats"), and investor presentations at conferences. An especially progressive feature enables individual investors to submit questions to management, the answers to which are published online in organized forums (a.k.a. "town hall meetings").

- Extending this concept further leads to virtual roadshows, whereby a company's management team updates members of the sell side and buy side on the current state of the business via interactive audio and video simulcasts. Group meetings can be repackaged for Webcast access by individual investors.

- As corporate IR programs focus attention on retail outreach and communications, more companies are developing direct stock purchase plans. E-commerce on the Internet bypasses the retail broker, making it easy and cost-effective for the individual to buy stock.

These points are but a few of many considerations for the planning and execution of Web-enabled IR. It is important to keep in mind that the Internet is a tool for the enhancement—not replacement—of fundamental practices. Face-to-face and voice communications between company executives and institutional money managers still form the fiber of investor relations.

CASE STUDY: A NEW ERA OF MESSAGE DELIVERY

Written by Stefanie Hein-Wells, who has worked in the public relations field industry for the past ten years. She is currently an account executive for Business Wire.

As we move forward into the twenty-first century, recent advances in technology have given amateur publicity seekers and seasoned public relations professionals a completely new venue to explore. Public relations is no longer only for the Fortune 500 and business press. With the development of the Internet, all types of businesses are looking to broadcast their messages to the general public. Today, technology is forcing PR practitioners to change how press releases are written, where they will be sent, and who will have access to them.

Since the development of the Internet, the PR field has not altered that dramatically, but that is about to change. Forecasts have shown that by the year 2003, Internet commerce could hit over $3 trillion and represent 5 percent of the world's economy. A paradigm shift of how the world can communicate has already occurred in the minds of the general public. The Internet has created a new medium of communications that offers not only traditional ways of receiving information, such as fax or telephone, but also multimedia type information at a very low cost.

PR professionals are also able to take advantage of this new medium. No longer are they confined to sending text over a wire service. With the development of the World Wide Web, PR professionals are able to include within their press release streaming video, audio, photos, charts, spreadsheets, and presentations.

Internet technology changed not only what PR can send out but also who will be receiving these press releases. In traditional public relations, press releases were written to be seen only by the business and trade press and financial analysts. This is no longer the case. Now any person with access to the Internet has the ability to view a press release from any company. This should drive the quality of press releases to a higher level. Although there will always be editors and journalists, PR professionals will no longer be able to depend on them to rewrite raw information before the public sees it.

Another industry that will need to change with the times are the conventional wire services. These services traditionally have given PR professionals access to the business and trade editors, as well as the financial analysts. As this new niche of direct communication emerges, the wire services will also need to adapt. Michael Lissauer of Business Wire, the global leader in news distribution, recognizes this: "Business Wire is both an innovative and pragmatic company. We have always been ahead of the curve in introducing new products and services to our members and in embracing technology. Business Wire has always provided the fastest baud rate in the commercial news wire industry. Our award winning website—businesswire.com—was the first such site to post all member news releases and to embed multimedia elements into the conventional news release. We will continue to make innovations to better serve our members." If wire services do not take this approach, they will no longer be able to exist.

The landscape of communications has undeniably changed dramatically in the last few years. As a result, PR professionals need to modify their modus operandi. The Internet will continue to give companies access to the press and to their potential customers. Skilled PR professionals need to adapt to both technology and their audience.

CASE STUDY: COMMUNICATIONS IN A HIGH-TECH WORLD

Written by Maura FitzGerald, president and CEO of FitzGerald Communications, a high-technology communications agency, who has more than 20 years of experience in journalism and public relations. As a former journalist and freelance writer, Maura's work has appeared in The Boston Globe, The Fort Lauderdale News, The Miami Herald,and USA Today.

In the rush to bring new products to market, many high-technology companies neglect to consider all the communication elements critical to carving out a unique value proposition in a crowded and noisy marketplace. This tendency toward an ad hoc approach to implementing communications programs is understandable given the pace of evolution and the fierce competition for market leadership. A few effective, well orchestrated techniques, however, can propel organizations, even those with unknown brands, ahead of stronger competitors in the high-technology race.

First, organizations must craft a set of strong corporate messages that transcends the products and that helps to create a clear corporate image in the minds of all target audiences. To cut through the noise in the industry, both corporate and product messages must be targeted, crisp, and consistent. Vehicles for reaching the desired audiences need to be mapped out, with the understanding of how the Internet allows immediate access to information by all audiences. Opinion leaders must be cultivated. Simultaneously, the company's executives need to have a dialogue with the industry about their point of view, whether it be standards, technology vision, changing business models, or management techniques.

Many companies in high-technology spend too much time focusing on products and not enough time on corporate identity. This is a mistake. Unfortunately, not all products are guaranteed to be the next paradigm-busting solution. The establishment of a corporate identity not only positions a company clearly and consistently to target audiences, such as the investment community (particularly important in a pending IPO situation), but also establishes a presence for the company that transcends its product line. Such an identity can eliminate the risk of a corporate downspin should one product launch fizzle, instead of ignite.

Messages regarding the company and products need to be crafted with end-user benefits in mind. Within technology, it is easy to fall into technical babble, but it is much more compelling to highlight the effect of a product on a customer's bottom line. The effectiveness of focusing on user benefits is a major reason why customer references and case studies are so crucial for high-technology companies.

In the development of messages, it is also important to keep in mind the audiences to which the messages are directed. A company may have several constituencies that it is trying to influence. These audiences might include such varied targets as the investment and online communities as well as press and industry analysts. Each of these audiences has different hot buttons; therefore, each message must be crafted carefully to effectively influence these varying mindsets.

Written messages and consistent external outreach are not the only outlets for influencing target audiences. Understanding these audiences and keeping track of their interests is critical. For example, companies should determine what conferences they attend and then attend them or speak at them. Additionally, they should be sensitive to audience requirements. For example, press contacts are always in need of user and analyst references. An organization savvy to this point provides such press contacts with user reference information before it is requested. They also cultivate analyst relationships within their respective space to offer them as resources.

No company can execute a successful communications campaign without involvement from senior executives. In the high-technology world where a vision for the future is a key element for success, it is imperative for executives, ideally CEOs, to make their marks on the industry. Such a "thought leader" campaign can be orchestrated in many ways: through bylined articles, speaking opportunities, and voicing opinions about critical news events. In the end, this voice sets the tone for the organization, but the communications professional must ensure that this voice is heard.

CASE STUDY: PROMOTING YOURSELF—AN INTEGRATED MIX OF WEB, PRINT, AND PEOPLE

Written by Kristi Swensson, professional actor and voice artist, who has been acting for more than a decade. She has appeared in such films as Inventing the Abbotts. She has also appeared on stage and in numerous radio and television commercials and corporate videos.

When you think about "Hollywood"—traditional movies and television—you acknowledge that technology is truly revolutionizing the entertainment industry. Computers are not only helping to produce the most incredible special effects and entire movies themselves, but they are also impacting the industry on a more personal level. As a professional actor and voice artist, I use technology to dramatically increase my ability to get work.

Today, I use what I like to call an *interactive résumé* on my website (www.kristiswensson.com). The site offers visitors my most updated resume, headshots, and audio and video clips of my radio, film, and television work. With the click of a mouse, visitors are able to see my entire portfolio and learn everything they need to about me. Because it's on the Web, I can easily update it as often as I like.

My website is linked to all of the different search engines. If you go to Yahoo! or Lycos and type in actor, my name would come up. My website contains a list of keywords you would type in if you were looking for someone like me. I have listed my name, actor, voice artist, actress, singer, voiceover, voice talent, and almost all combinations of words that might pertain to the entertainment industry. As a result, my name pops up a lot and I get auditions and available jobs.

I must point out, though, that my website is just one element of a totally integrated approach I take to secure new acting and voiceover opportunities. I have a print ad that I run every year in the *Real Directory* (an annual publication that contains information about actors, agents, casting directors, stunt people, and production companies in the San Francisco Bay area.) The *Real Directory* is sent, free of charge, to 2,000 local corporations. The print ad has a headshot and, of course, my Web address. I also have an agent who has copies of my audio and video demo tapes, headshots, and résumés that she sends out via snail mail. All of these elements—traditional and technological—help me expand my audience and reach people who might never hear of me.

The entertainment industry is just now starting to embrace the Internet as a way to save time and energy, especially when looking for talent. Many casting companies are now coming up with websites where actors can post their résumés and headshots. The actors pay a small fee to post, which enables the site to remain free for directors and casting directors who are looking to fill roles. The key advantage is time. With the site's search capabilities, they can enter specifics about the actor they want. They can sort the headshots and résumés by type, age, race, hair color, or look. If the actors they select have streaming audio or video clips, they can speed up the process even more by not having to call their agents, request demo tapes and wait for the mail.

The use of technology to enhance careers or seek new business is not limited to the acting profession. This type of integrated mix—the Web, traditional media, and the personal touch—is already being used in fields such as human resources, sales, fundraising, politics, public relations, and advertising. It has opened up a global audience and enabled me to take charge of my career.

CASE STUDY: NASA PUBLIC AFFAIRS' GIANT LEAP TO HIGH-TECH

Written by Lisa Malone, APR, who has more than 17 years' experience in public relations and was NASA's first female space shuttle launch commentator. As chief of NASA's media services office, she plans, implements, and oversees activities for the thousands of U.S. and international media representatives who attend each of the space shuttle and expendable vehicle launches each year.

As a government public affairs professional for nearly two decades, I have experienced first hand the way technology can dramatically change your daily life. When I first joined the NASA News Department at Kennedy Space Center, as an intern in the early 1980s, I used to help stuff "hot" news releases into hundreds of envelopes for distribution to the news media. Someone in the office would volunteer to make a mad dash to the post office before it closed so that the media could get the releases quickly. At that time, we had only a few old clunky computers in the office and had to take turns using them to write our stories about NASA's accomplishments.

As technology advanced, we moved on to hand-faxing individual releases to space reporters as a supplement to snail mail. Our clerical help was consumed with standing over the fax machine trying to distribute the news. We later discovered that our faxes could be simultaneously sent or "broadcasted" to multiple phone numbers. Then, in the early 1990s, the Internet became the clear choice of vehicles to communicate our message in a timely manner. It truly revolutionized the manner in which we distributed information. We now post all news releases and press kits to our website and use list servers to distribute video news events of the day, news releases, and status reports. This information is automatically deposited into the e-mail accounts of subscribing reporters and other constituents.

Still photographs are now put into a digital format and posted to the Web immediately after a shuttle launch. Our statistics show that the photo section of the Web routinely receives one of the highest amounts of hits. We also give newspaper and wire photographers a disk of selected images instead of eight-by-ten glossy prints. These technologies enable NASA to easily distribute hundreds of photographs to publications all over the world.

Since the beginning of human space flight in the early 1960s, television has always been an important ingredient in the space agency's recipe for conveying information to the public. Those grainy images and muffled voices coming back from the moon during the Apollo program have evolved into continuous round-the-clock coverage of all space shuttle launches, missions, and landings. Now, reporters on the ground are even allowed to ask questions of astronauts while they float around inside the shuttle during the routine "in-flight" news conference.

Many other NASA stories are aired via satellite several times a day from headquarters, which collects video packages from the ten different NASA field centers around the country. These stories are packed with sound bites from experts and feature spectacular images on topics such as the latest Mars mission, new discoveries from the Hubble Space Telescope, new technologies that can make flying in a commercial aircraft safer, or an analysis of threatening hurricanes. Many television stations around the country use these stories from the daily NASA television feed. Many can't afford to send news crews to Florida for each launch, so the space agency also conducts hundreds of live shots, via satellite, from various NASA centers. On launch day, several astronauts conduct as many as 50 live shots to stations around the country.

The public affairs department has become more media savvy in the last few years with its concerted effort to improve the quality of the products we offer to the media and public. We have tried to eliminate acronyms and NASA jargon and use catchier angles for stories. We've refined the quality of television products with the use of pertinent backdrops, articulate experts, and spectacular animation and deliver it to the media via satellite during their broadcast times. All organizations within NASA have Web pages to help educate the public about their specific programs. A tremendous effort is being made to keep the information updated and timely.

In the future, I expect we'll become even more technology savvy in communicating NASA's various stories. We are developing enhanced features for Web services such as more refined video streaming, audio sound bites, animation, and so forth. We are also in the initial stages of defining our needs for high-definition television to meet future industry standards. With technology, the general public can bypass the traditional means of communications altogether. They can surf the Web and instantly find space information unfiltered by the news media. They don't even have to call a NASA center to ask for a brochure. NASA's use of the Internet and live satellite coverage are communications tools that have substantially increased the public's understanding of NASA science and technology programs.

CASE STUDY: A PRINT JOURNALIST'S PERSPECTIVE

Written by Doug Levy, who has covered technology, science, and health for USA Today and United Press International. He was a producer for NBC Radio/Westwood One, worked at National Public Radio, and was an assistant director in the public affairs office of Johns Hopkins Medical Institutions. He is currently senior editor of health and pharmacy information for PlanetRx.com, an online pharmacy and health company.

Technology is both the bane of my existence and what I live for. The ever-increasing modes of communication mean that public relations people don't just call or write, now they call, write, fax, and e-mail. Some even find my pager number and misuse that. As a technology journalist, I am constantly amazed at how few people step back and really think about how they are using technology to make their jobs more effective. The vast majority of public relations agencies are sending out the same junk mail that used to waste stamps via e-mail—mass mailings that have nothing to do with my publication or what I cover. Such spam is worthless, ineffective, and annoying. The really smart PR people come up with ways to use technology to make things better. Simple stuff, like keeping a database of reporters and knowing what stories they've done—and using it to tailor pitches better.

Among the cooler technologies to come into my life recently are those that help me manage communications. Caller ID helps me tell whether I'm getting a phone call from a hard-to-reach CEO or from yet another flack pitching yet another product launch or new website. Eventually, everything will be linked together so that voice mail, e-mail, faxes, and whatever other kinds of communication we dream up can go into one "in box." Unified messaging really will make a difference once the technology is perfected, or at least good enough to be truly reliable. This new technology has positive aspects, too. The dozens of companies trying to get unified messaging right makes my job exciting—both because I know it will improve my life and because it will be a great story to cover.

The intense competition in Silicon Valley and other technology centers is unmatched in our history. Companies that stumble crumble, whereas those that execute well become runaway leaders until someone else with a better idea comes along. It's fascinating to watch this jockeying for position, the rush to generate buzz, and the post-launch "prove-it-really-works" period. But it all boils down to using technology not for technology's sake but to satisfy a need. People buy books at Amazon.com because they're interested in reading in the first place. Amazon just makes it easier to make the purchase. I've seen pitch after pitch for "online press rooms" that expect me to take the time to register and then periodically check the site. Some even have the audacity to spam me with useless releases as a way of thanking me for registering. These are never going to appeal to daily newspaper reporters who are already swamped with story ideas and junk.

There is no secret to successful story placement, and it's not going to change dramatically as the technology moves ahead into the next millennium. Story pitches work because they are effectively targeted at the right person and the right publication and presented by someone who takes the time to prepare before calling. The existence of new software won't do anything to eliminate the junior PR person who calls to pitch a story that's already been in print. The best PR folks understand this, and I hope that their numbers grow.

CASE STUDY: NONPROFIT MARKETING

Written by Michelle Barnes, the director of marketing at Ramp Networks. A lifelong volunteer, she also serves on the boards of directors for several local (San Francisco Bay area) and national nonprofit organizations.

Thousands of nonprofits and charities market their causes and services primarily to a local constituency. They are the most visible at the holidays when many people are looking at annual charitable contributions. But these organizations are actually working year-round, advancing their organization's mission. Advances in technology, particularly Internet technology, have opened a whole new way of marketing for them.

A nonprofit doesn't measure its success by profit and loss. It looks at its impact on the community, its ability to serve its constituents, its fundraising, and its ability to change thoughts and behavior. Although national organizations such as the Red Cross, the United Negro College Fund, and The Nature Conservancy have marketing budgets and annual campaigns, thousands of local nonprofits operate with no budget or staff, other than the efforts of their boards of directors and volunteers.

Six Steps to Nonprofit Marketing Planning

1. *Have a clear mission for the organization.* State it in writing. Review it often. Put your mission statement on every communication.

2. *Information is your most powerful tool.* Keep a computer database of donors, volunteers, and other supporters. In this database, track contact information as well as the types of contribu-

tions (for example, time, money, resources, ideas) people want to contribute. Use a website to keep them informed about special appeals and the work of the organization.

3. *Communicate often and everywhere.* Make sure that your organization, mission, and current needs are getting as much play as possible. Keep the local media informed. Keep national organizations informed (if you are local) and your local affiliates (if you are national).

4. *Expand your team every day.* Local journalists will often cover "special interest stories." Local celebrities and sports heroes will also lend their names, time, and leadership to help charities. Local businesses are also renowned for donating products, services, and resources to help promote causes for which they believe. Many advertising and PR firms will do pro bono work for a cause their employees support. Don't forget pro bono professional services and consulting. Many organizations will print, distribute, and so forth at "cost" if the charity is interesting to them. Leverage your impact by asking more people to be on the team. People love to be asked to help and everyone has a contribution to make. Let them.

5. *Take full advantage of the Internet.* Seriously consider having a website that gives at least basic information about your organization. This site can be as simple as a home page with contact information and a mission statement. Having a registration page to let visitors sign up for more information will help you expand your team. Consider asking a budding website developer to design a site for you. It's good publicity for both parties. Directing supporters to your website is also a great way to keep in touch. Use this as the vehicle to promote your suppliers. Put your website address on all communications. All of these suggestions further establish the credibility of the organization as well as leverage a technology most people already use.

6. *Have a clear call to action.* When people want to be part of your mission, tell them exactly what they can do. Have a variety of options so you can include everyone in your campaigns. A donation form should be included in all communications. Always list a phone number and have someone available who can take the call. Have an e-mail address and respond promptly.

Marketing at a nonprofit is exciting, challenging, and rewarding. Many people with for-profit backgrounds can make the transition by volunteering at a local charity as a way to get started. Using simple technology such as the Internet and the Web can help any organization increase communications and expand its team easily and efficiently.

CASE STUDY: THE MARKETING GAME

Written by Todd Johnson, vice president of worldwide marketing for BackWeb Technologies. Prior to joining BackWeb, he held various senior-executive positions at Silicon Graphics corporation, now SGI. His experiences have ranged from running product marketing to managing the restructure of all marketing efforts for a $3 billion company.

The impact of technology on marketing is much the same as the impact of technology on golf. At the end of the day the game is still the same. Golf—hit the small ball across grass and ultimately into the hole. Marketing—the process of creating a differentiated position in the market and driving that position, and ultimately demand, by emphasizing consistency, reach, and frequency of the message to your target audience. Graphite shafts and titanium club heads have changed the process of getting the ball to the hole, and the Internet has changed the process of getting your message to the market.

So, what's different? Time is accelerated. My friend Jim Clark, founder of SGI, Netscape, and Healtheon, has written a book called *Netscape Time*. The title is very telling. In fact, the Internet has changed all aspects of how time is measured and how marketing has to be approached. Prior to the Internet, products were regularly announced in serial fashion one continent at a time. U.S. companies, especially technology companies, made it standard procedure to announce products in the Americas, then a quarter later in Europe, and a quarter later in Asia. Today, information available through the Internet is not bound by physical or political boundaries. Global announcements have become a necessity. This literally shortens product life cycles.

Our economy is increasingly moving toward a build-to-order model, thus no inventory sits in the channel. More commerce is taking place directly between the manufacturer and the buyer. This reduction in distribution steps is again shortening the cycle. There is this company run by a guy named Michael Dell—but I guess you already know the story. His model is not reserved for PCs; this model will be common across most product categories.

It is a global market. Even in a simple example, the Internet has changed the nature of pricing products. Long ago, companies could set varying prices for different locations around the globe. Today, not only do customers get visibility to pricing schemes through the Web, in most cases they can locate distribution options via the Internet that may be located across the globe.

Pricing differentials are quickly boiling down to only the difference in freight, duty, and insurance costs for different locations. Internet commerce also enables even the smallest company to become a global supplier.

With technology, brands will become more important and less important. Yes, more choices will be available in all product categories, but consumers will be increasingly attracted to a set of primary brands that have acquired mindshare and established distribution agreements with key Internet retailers. Small-town shoppers and big-city shoppers will share the same electronic marketplaces. Competition for "virtual shelf space" with the prime distributors will be tougher than ever. Globally, large e-retailers will be fewer in number than today's "storefront" world, but each will drive much higher volumes. Big brands will use economies of scale and their already established franchise positions to drive both pricing and availability advantage. But brands will become less important in the supply chain. Companies will have access to suppliers who will be able to bid electronically for contracts. Cost, quality, and timely delivery will be the drivers for purchases. Brands will mean less; performance will mean more.

So, where does this leave us? Like golf, the marketing game is still the same, but the methods and the tools that impact the particulars have changed dramatically. The pace is faster, the competition is broader, and the playing field is more level. But, like golf, regardless of the power of the tools, talent and hard work will prevail. After all, we play the game for fun don't we?

FREE STUFF AND OTHER RESOURCES

Whether you are a novice public relations or marketing practitioner or a seasoned veteran of the two fields, you can benefit from a wide assortment of free stuff and other resources that are available either through the Web or through traditional outlets. This chapter should serve as a guide to help you find everything from free banner exchange networks to professional media training. If you're interested in a category for which I don't provide information, then please feel free to contact me at skohl@sierracomm.com.

FREE STUFF

Banner Creation

HyperBanner (www.hyperbanner.com) has created a tool designed to help small businesses quickly and easily develop website banners. Its product, QuickBanner, offers complete banner creation for developing professional, high-quality banner advertisements in minutes. It provides templates that are specialized for different target audiences and optimized for maximum visibility. Banner creators do not need professional graphics or Web training to use QuickBanner. The QuickBanner tool is free.

Banner Exchange Networks

SmartAge.com (www.smartage.com) offers the free SmartClicks banner advertising creator and free banner exchange network that is designed especially for small and growing businesses. You show network members' banners on your website, and they show your ads on theirs. For every two banner impressions you show, one banner credit is awarded to you. You may also receive a weekly newsletter on building and promoting your website.

Web-Based Meeting Service

WebEx.com (www.webex.com) is the world's first free Web-based meeting service. WebEx is the first service to enable sophisticated, real-time visual and verbal interaction across the Web that requires only an ordinary browser and a telephone. WebEx enables spontaneous sharing of documents, presentations, Web content, and applications.

Streaming Technology

QuickTime 4 by Apple (www.apple.com/quicktime) lets you add more than 200 digital media capabilities and components to your Mac or PC for free.

Real Networks (www.realnetworks.com) offers the RealPlayer G2 for free. It plays all Real content and allows you to access live and on-demand audio and video.

HotMedia (www.ibm.com/hotmedia) is a toolkit for creative professionals to enrich e-business applications with rich media. With HotMedia, you can add special effects, such as streaming audio, 360-degree views, animations, panning and scrolling, and zoomable multiresolution images. Add interactions and hot links, and assemble the entire experience into one file, easily added to a Web page and delivered over today's networks.

Newsletters

Internet World News (www.internetworldnews.com) is a free daily e-zine that reports recent Internet developments of interest to the online community.

Search Engine Watch (www.searchenginewatch.com) is a free monthly e-newsletter with information about search engine companies. This is a good source of information for the behind-the-scenes operations of search engines.

ClickZ (www.clickz.com) is the leading business-to-business daily online newsletter covering the business of Internet marketing and advertising. Included in its network is an extensive archive of ClickZ pieces and a resource directory.

Emarketer (www.emarketer.com) is a comprehensive, objective resource of what's happening with e-business. It is an easy-to-use, one-stop resource—a dependable business tool for anyone setting up or operating a business online. You can register on the site to receive a free weekly newsletter, full of eMarketer news highlights, statistics, and other hot tidbits.

Sierra Communications (www.sierracomm.com) offers free monthly public relations and marketing tips on its Web site that encompass everything from how to court the nation's top-tier business press, to getting your CEO invited to appear on CNBC. Sierracomm specializes in Internet, technology, general consumer, education, and aerospace public relations. Its strengths lie in media relations, press materials and marketing collateral development, and above all, creativity. Its campaigns have won numerous public relations and marketing awards in both California and Florida.

◆ ALMOST FREE

Electronic Library (www.electroniclibrary.com) provides access to thousands of full-text newspapers, magazines, extensive photo archives, and complete encyclopedias for an annual fee of $59.95.

SmartAge Watch (www.smartage.com/watch) is a 24-hour website monitoring and alert service for small businesses that don't have the budgets to support an MIS staff. For $6.95 per month, SmartAge Watch assures small and growing businesses that their websites are up and running and alerts site owners to server problems via e-mail.

The *Wall Street Journal* (www.wsj.com), the *New York Times* (www.nytimes.com), and the *San Jose Mercury News* (www.sjmercury.com) all have terrific story archives. You can conduct a search for free, but you have to pay to download the entire article. Costs vary from two to four dollars per article.

FaxProfiles™ is a database of more than 4,000 current biographies of editors and journalists across the United States. FaxProfiles covers a wide range of publications, beats, and locations. Profiles generally run under $100 and can either be faxed or e-mailed to you. Call 1-888-FAXPROFILES or visit PR Newswire (www.prnewswire.com) for more information.

◆ OTHER RESOURCES

Wire Services

Business Wire (www.businesswire.com) is one of the leading sources of news on major U.S. corporations, including Fortune 1000 and Nasdaq companies. The company electronically disseminates full-text news releases for public and investor relations professionals simultaneously to the news media, the Internet, online services and databases, and the investment community worldwide.

PR Newswire (www.prnewswire.com) is the world's leader in the electronic delivery of news releases and information directly from companies, institutions, and agencies to the media, financial community, and consumers. PR Newswire's services begin with NewsLines and include broadcast fax and fax-on-demand applications, delivery by e-mail, photo transmission, Internet services, and more.

Dow Jones Newswires (www.dowjones.com/newswires) is a news wire service that has been a reliable and leading source of financial news for more than 100 years. More than 3,500 editors and reporters in more than 250 markets worldwide transmit an average of 5,000 news items every day. To find out where to submit your press release, please e-mail newswires@dowjones.com.

Reuters (www.reuters.com) is another news wire service that claims to be the world's-largest distributor of real-time financial data, with information going to more than 450,000 users. Visit www.reuters.com/contacts/editor.htm to find the proper contact for submitting your news.

Bloomberg (www.bloomberg.com) is powered by more than 80 news bureaus. Bloomberg's award-winning news service delivers top stories from financial markets in the United States and around the world. Included in this section are reports on the latest developments in the high-tech industry, as well as Bloomberg's star lineup of columnists. Visit www.bloomberg.com/products/usnews.html to find out how to submit your news.

Research

GartnerGroup (www.gartnergroup.com) is touted as the world's leading authority on information technology, providing clients with a wide range of products and services in the areas of advisory services, measurement, market research, decision support, analysis, and consulting. GartnerGroup press releases are a good source of free statistics as long as you attribute the information to the organization.

Yankee Group (www.yankeegroup.com), a subsidiary of Primark Corporation, is an internationally recognized leader in information technology research and advisory services, focusing on strategic planning assistance, technology forecasting, and industry analysis. Yankee Group press releases are a good source of free statistics as long as you attribute the information to the organization.

Forrester Research (www.forrester.com) is a leading independent research firm that analyzes technology change and its impact on business, consumers, and society. Forrester's press releases are a good source of free statistics as long as you attribute the information to the organization.

IDG (www.idg.com) is the world's leading information technology media, research, and exposition company. Founded in 1964, IDG had 1998 revenues of $2.35 billion and has more than 9,000 employees worldwide. IDG offers the widest range of media options, which reach 90 million buyers in 75 countries, representing 95 percent of worldwide information technology spending. IDG press releases are a good source of free statistics as long as you attribute the information to the organization.

Estats (www.estats.com) is a online repository of free statistics and for-purchase reports on e-commerce, the Web, ad revenues, demographics, retail, and other interesting categories. This site is updated daily with new information.

Editorial Calendars

EdCals.com (www.edcals.com) is a subscription-based website for public relations, advertising, media, and marketing novices and professionals. Subscribers can search thousands of continuously updated editorial calendars that contain more than 100,000 upcoming stories and special issues from nearly every leading U.S. magazine and newspaper. You also receive "What's New?" bulletins that let you know every relevant change personally via a custom e-mail service.

Web Design

Flamingo Software Company has more than six years of expertise in website design and construction. Other services include search engine registrations and maintenance;

website statistics and analysis tools; e-commerce solutions; auction site development and hosting; creative consulting; graphic design and animation; and streaming video and media services. For information, visit www.flamingo-software.com or call 407/267-3261.

Public Relations Firms

Sierra Communications (www.sierracomm.com) specializes in Internet, technology, general consumer, education, and aerospace public relations. Sierracomm's strengths lie in media relations, press materials, and marketing collateral development, and above all, creativity. Its campaigns have won numerous public relations and marketing awards in California and Florida.

FitzGerald Communications, Inc.(www.fitzgerald.com) provides strategic corporate communications counsel, including corporate image visibility, product and service promotion, investor relations, and interactive communications to high-technology companies spanning a wide range of market segments. The Cambridge, Massachusetts–based agency has offices in Arlington, Virginia, and San Francisco, California. FitzGerald can be reached through the Web or by phone at 617/494-9500.

Strategic Communications Group (www.scg1.com) is an integrated marketing communications and public relations agency serving clients in the technology, software, Internet, and telecommunications markets. Strategic can be reached through the Web or by phone at 301/408-4500.

Gail Bergman PR is a Toronto-based public relations firm specializing in media relations, communications, and special events. Established in 1994, the company develops and executes public relations programs for a wide range of private and public organizations across Canada, with specific emphasis in the information technology field. Contact Gail Bergman, APR, at 905/886-1340 or via e-mail at gb_pr@pathcom.com.

Investor Relations

Demer IR Counsel, Inc., founded in 1989 and headquartered in the San Francisco Bay Area, offers a full range of investor relations services for public, private, and pre-IPO companies. As the only West Coast–based IR firm specializing in high-technology companies, Demer IR focuses clients on managing expectations to build market value. For more information, call 925/938-2678 or visit Demer's website at www.demer-ir.com.

Strategic Communication Consulting and Video Production

Nelson Communications, Inc. has been offering high-end video production and strategic communication consulting services since 1998. Based in Atlanta, NCI's clients include Novell, Procter & Gamble, The United Arab Emirates, and The Atlanta School Board. For more information, e-mail brian.nelson@worldnet.att.net.

Talent for Radio, TV, and Film

Kristi Swensson (www.kristiswensson.com) is a professional actor and voice artist who has appeared in such films as *Inventing the Abbotts* as well as in radio and television commercials and corporate videos. Contact her by visiting www.kristiswensson.com/contact.html or call 408/994-5715.

Search Engine Organizations

Search Engine Watch (www.searchenginewatch.com) reports that more than 73,000 readers depend on its free monthly newsletter to keep up with the search engines. Its website offers submission tips, such as using meta tags, improving placement, and how to submit URLs. It gives comparison reviews, information about which search engines are most popular, and results from various tests complete with statistics.

Search Engine Registration Software

Net Submitter Pro
(www.softwaresolutions.net./submitter.htm)

Cyberrat 2000 (www.dotit.com/2000/download.htm)

WebPosition Gold (www.praia.com/index.htm)

Popular Search Engines

Alta Vista (www.altavista.com)

Excite (www.excite.com)

Google (www.google.com)

HotBot (www.hotbot.com)

Infoseek (www.infoseek.com)

Lycos (www.lycos.com)

MSN Search (www.searchmsn.com)

Open Directory (www.dmoz.org)

Yahoo! (www.yahoo.com)

APPENDIX

For Immediate Release

Contact:
Name
Title
Organization
Phone
E-mail

Headline: The Headline Should Not Be in All Caps

San Jose, California—Month XX, 2000—Company ABC, a leading provider of something, today announced that

_____

_____. Mention the who, what, where, when, why, and how in this first paragraph. You may also want to include the benefits.

(Quote)

"This product is the greatest thing since sliced bread," said Joe Smith, president of partner company, customer, or third party. "In addition, it offers great benefits to our customers, partners, and employees."

(More detailed description of company, product, service, event, or activity.)

This book provides readers with the inside scoop on public relations and marketing. It offers them tips, information, on new technology, etc. Readers will further benefit from its_____.

(Quote from your company or organization)

"I am using this quote opportunity to talk about the big picture," said Mary Brown, CEO of Company ABC. "This is my chance to talk about my company's vision and leading position in the industry."

(Further explanation of company, product, service, event, or activity if needed)

This paragraph and additional paragraphs can be used to provide even more detailed information about the subject matter. Keep it very factual. Do not use industry buzzwords or hype of any kind in these paragraphs. This is the place where journalists can find specific information about the company, product, service, event. or activity.

(Boilerplate)

Company ABC is a leading provider of DEF. With more than XX offices worldwide, Company ABC does this and that. This is your company or organization's standard paragraph that is used at the end of all press releases. It's very important to decide exactly what these words will be and try to be consistent. Investors, especially, will check boilerplates to see if the company has changed its focus or key messages. This could be a red flag to investors.

###

(This symbol marks the end of the press release)

Place trademark information here, if necessary.

ABOUT THE AUTHOR

Susan Kohl, APR, is a veteran of high-tech public relations. She has worked in California's Silicon Valley since 1996 and in Florida's high-tech aerospace community for nearly a decade. Prior to her career in public relations, she worked as a radio and television news journalist for CBS Radio, WCPX-TV in Orlando, Florida, and KCOY-TV in Santa Maria, California. She also served as host for PM Magazine, Montana, and as a co-host for the 1984 March of Dimes telethon for South Central Montana.

Susan Kohl is the co-founder of Sierra Communications, a technology-oriented public relations and marketing firm. She has won numerous awards for her public relations and marketing efforts, and was recently accredited by the Public Relations Society of America. In addition, she was the founder and publisher of two national newsletters: *The West Coast Edition and Space Classroom News.* She also wrote, co-produced, and hosted the documentary *Apollo 11: 20 Years and Counting.*

Susan Kohl is a seasoned on-air personality. She holds a Bachelor of Arts degree from California State University, Chico.

◆ SIERRA COMMUNICATIONS

Susan Kohl, author of *Getting Attention: Leading-Edge Lessons for Publicity and Marketing,* is the co-founder of Sierra Communications, a technology-oriented public relations and marketing firm. Sierra Communications offers a wide variety of services that include media relations, marketing collateral development, strategic planning for public relations and marketing activities, and website development. The Sierra Communications team specializes in Internet, high-tech, aerospace, and consumer-related public relations and marketing activities. It also has expertise in pre–initial public offering (IPO) publicity and marketing.

If you would like more information about Sierra Communications, please contact Susan Kohl, APR, at skohl@sierracomm.com. You may also visit the Sierra Communications Web site at www.sierracomm.com to learn more about its services and staff. The site offers free monthly publicity and marketing tips that can help you further your business success. It also offers exclusive public relations and marketing case studies, professional workbooks, and informational briefing sheets.

INDEX